ESSAYS

IN LOGIC

From ARISTOTLE to RUSSELL

PRENTICE-HALL INTERNATIONAL, INC., *London*
PRENTICE-HALL OF AUSTRALIA, PTY., LTD., *Sydney*
PRENTICE-HALL OF CANADA, LTD., *Toronto*
PRENTICE-HALL FRANCE, S.A.R.L., *Paris*
PRENTICE-HALL OF JAPAN, INC., *Tokyo*
PRENTICE-HALL DE MEXICO, S.A., *Mexico City*

ESSAYS

IN LOGIC

From ARISTOTLE to RUSSELL

Selected
and
Edited by
RONALD JAGER
Northwestern University

PRENTICE-HALL, INC.
Englewood Cliffs, N.J.

Current printing (last digit):

12 11 10 9 8 7 6 5 4 3

LIBRARY OF CONGRESS CATALOG CARD NO.

63-7922

PRINTED IN THE UNITED STATES OF AMERICA
28352-C

PREFACE

The arguments favoring the study of philosophers' original texts, whether by student or amorphous "general reader," are manifold and overwhelming. Fortunately, the revival of the practice coincides, as cause and consequent, with a paper-backed publishing revolution which makes it possible for most of us to own Aristotle's or Russell's books if we wish. What the reader has in hand, however, is only a substitute for that. Substitute and prologue, but it aims to serve better than available textbook alternatives.

In the colleges, increased use of original texts is widespread in such branches of philosophy as epistemology and ethics. Pedagogically, at least, logic has lagged behind. One reason may lie in the fearsome difficulty of some of the important sources. But not everything that Aristotle wrote is as obscure as the popular conviction suggests, nor, for that matter, as archaic as Russell, for one, believes. In any event, the intention of the present book is to confront the reader with significant texts which are not beyond the disciplined reach of the first year logic student.

Further reason for the pedagogical logical lag lies perhaps in the prevalence of a professional attitude which tends to regard logic and its history, like some of science, as the accumulation of results on the frontier, rather than a continuing debate on the fundamentals. Though Russell is more or less an exponent of this view, it has the consequence that the texts of both Russell and Aristotle are widely taken to be as *pedagogically* dispensable as those of, say, Einstein or Newton. We can let the case of Newton and Einstein rest; but the conviction that such an attitude is inappropriate with respect to Aristotle, Russell, and the rest is what inspires the present collection.

There are plenty of imperfections in this assembly, faults not only of the collected, but of the collecting. So let us offer the kindly critic a helping hand, and observe that what is here represented

v

may be too little, too one-sided, too dated. It can scarcely be helped. There can be no pretension to historical adequacy in a few hundred pages; so, for example, the Stoics, the Mediaevals, and the Idealists had to be left aside. And there can be no hope for mutual relevance without one-sidedness; so, for example, the syllogism, in attack and defense, tends to dominate the scene. And there can be no hope for historical depth without the risk of obscurantism; so, concerned for the depth and accepting the risk, we exclude the elegant systems of present-day mathematical logic. But to request instruction from yesterday is not to despise today. The instruction lies in history's dialogue on the underpinnings of formal logic: the nature, the value, and the justification of this logic in its reciprocal contact with the claims of philosophy on the one hand and the requirements of the common life on the other.

Ronald Jager

CONTENTS

ESSAYS

IN LOGIC

From ARISTOTLE to RUSSELL

ARISTOTLE

(384-322 B.C.)

He was "the master of those who knew," said Dante. He was
born in Stagira, a Greek colonial town on the shores of the Aegean,
the son of a physician in the Macedonian court. When a scholar of seven-
teen Aristotle went to Athens to study at the famous Academy of Plato. For
twenty years he remained with his master, but on Plato's death in 347 B.C.
he went to Asia Minor where he married, continued to conduct research,
and (as was only recently established) to write philosophy. For a time he
was a tutor in the court of Pella to a young prince remembered later in
history as Alexander the Great. When in his late forties, Aristotle returned
to Athens, founded his own school, the Lyceum, and remained as its head
for about twelve years. During this time he gathered about him a brilliant
and productive group of scientists and philosophers, and wrote original
treatises in practically every domain of knowledge.

When Alexander the Great died in 323 B.C., Aristotle glanced at the
gathering political storm, hurriedly put his school and his papers in the
charge of a friend, and, with a keen memory of Socrates, quit Athens for
the isle of Euboea—reportedly commenting that he did not want "Athens
to sin twice against philosophy." Aristotle's hurried concern that Athens
remain virtuous by not killing him kept him from putting his accumulat-
ing manuscripts into finished order and so bequeathed to classicists a happy
scholarly hunting ground.

One of the hunted items, and the only one of pertinence here, is
Aristotle's precise conception of logic and the order and relevance of his
several manuscripts on the subject. Of such manuscripts, it appeared that
there were six in all, none of them called "Logic." Indeed, that word does
not seem to be in Aristotle's philosophical vocabulary, though he did give
us many of the terms in which we still discuss the subject. We know his
books by their English names: *Categories, On Interpretation, Prior Analytics, Posterior Analytics, Topics,* and *Sophistical Refutations.* It was not
Aristotle but his commentators of 500 years later who referred to the six
books together as *Organon* (instrument).

Thus was fashioned the first—and, in the eyes of many philosophers,

1

the best—textbook on logic: six treatises, written at different times, for different purposes and audiences, treating and re-treating a variety of fundamental but criss-crossing themes with the rigor and originality of sure genius. He began and finished the subject, said Kant.

At least he began it. And he began too the dispute as to the boundaries of logic and its relation to the rest of philosophy and life. Two competing traditions, and countless variations on them, claim his authority. Roughly expressed, the traditions, which may be called those of formal and of material logic, hold: (a) that logic is a purely formal study of valid thought, which ideally can be abstracted from all content and subject matter; and, (b) that logic concerns thought and reasoning only as expressing reality and that thus the instruments of reasoning and the reality known cannot be conceived separably. Aristotle himself may well have changed his mind on the question, or possibly rejected the distinction; we cannot be certain. Moreover, it is difficult to find a place for the whole of logic in the system of the sciences as Aristotle has defined and divided them, namely, the theoretical, the practical, and the productive. Doubtless he would have taken logic to be the "organon," the instrument and precondition of the study of the arts and sciences.

It is from Aristotle that we derive what the tradition has called the "three principles of logic," or "the laws of thought"—Identity, Excluded Middle, Non-contradiction. But Aristotle himself never got around to working out their precise relation to the rest of his logic, and, indeed, discussed them more in his Metaphysics than elsewhere. Thus it is worthwhile to present these important principles here in his own words. Identity: "Whatever is true, must agree with itself in every respect." Excluded Middle: "Between the terms of a contradictory opposition, there can be nothing in the middle; we must necessarily either affirm or deny everything of everything else." Non-contradiction: "The same thing cannot possibly be true and not true of the same thing and in the same respect." It is a worthy exercise for the reader to study the relevance of these principles to the ensuing pages.

Aristotle's numerous detailed investigations are far too extensive to summarize, but a few specific statements in orientation to the following selections are in order.

On Interpretation is a study of the various units of thought, though Aristotle's chief preoccupation is the composition and relation of propositions. The classification of propositions is somewhat different from that in *Prior Analytics,* and the familiar doctrine of distribution, though used, is not expounded. He does, however, treat what has been known in the tradition as the Square of Opposition and Immediate Inference. The less difficult portions of his discussion of these have been included here. The famous interlude on the "sea battle tomorrow," though it raises profound questions (treated today in a special branch of philosophy called modal logic), is included for historical interest.

Prior Analytics presents Aristotle's theory of the syllogism in its moods and figures. There seems to be no room here for the singular judgment in a syllogism, nor is any use made of the fourth figure. Both of these are familiar to the logical tradition, and their absence here, as well as the emphasis on the Perfect Figure, are very important consequences of Aristotle's further philosophical theory.

Posterior Analytics is, in effect, Aristotle's philosophy of science. It contains an elaboration of syllogistic thinking, including its application to scientific demonstration, then an elaboration of the latter, including its presuppositions and methods. Of this work, only a short section, which deals with causes, essential natures, and definition, is presented.

Topics is clearly an assembly of various documents, some of which seem to be written in complete independence of the doctrine of the syllogism. Of special interest and of vast historical importance are the doctrines of "Categories" and "Predicables" which are here adumbrated. The "Predicables" concern the ways in which a predicate may be related to a subject. The discussion here reproduced turns out to have been exploratory and to give way in Book IV to the version (too complicated for inclusion) which subsequently passed into mediaeval philosophy, namely, *genus, species, differentia, proprium,* and *accidens.* The "Categories" concerns the classes of predicates, being at once a distinction between ways of thinking and of things thought about. The list of categories is here somewhat different from that in the work by that name—from which latter work, incidentally, no selection is here included.

Sophistical Refutations is a study of the fallacies of reasoning, using two broad classifications: fallacies which depend on language and those which do not. At the conclusion, Aristotle frankly lays claim to having founded the subject of logic.

ON INTERPRETATION[1]

*   *   *

17ª

Every sentence has meaning, not as being the natural means by which a physical faculty is realized, but, as we have said, by convention. Yet every sentence is not a proposition; only such are propositions as have in them either truth or falsity. Thus a prayer is a sentence, but is neither true nor false.

5   Let us therefore dismiss all other types of sentence but the proposition, for this last concerns our present inquiry, whereas the investigation of the others belongs rather to the study of rhetoric or of poetry.

The first class of simple propositions is the simple affirmation, the next, the simple denial; all others are only one by conjunction.

10   Every proposition must contain a verb or the tense of a verb. The phrase which defines the species 'man,' if no verb in present, past, or future time be added, is not a proposition. It may be asked how the expression 'a footed animal with two feet' can be called single; for it is not the circumstance that the words follow in unbroken succession that effects the unity. This inquiry, however, finds its place in an investigation foreign to that before us.

15   We call those propositions single which indicate a single fact, or the conjunction of the parts of which results in unity: those propositions, on the other hand, are separate and many in number, which indicate many facts, or whose parts have no conjunction.

---

[1] The following selections are reprinted from *The Works of Aristotle,* Volume I, translated under the editorship of W. D. Ross. (London: Oxford University Press, 1928). Only some of the footnotes of the Ross edition are used. The marginal numbers refer, as is usual with Aristotle's texts, to the page, column, and line of the standard Berlin Academy Edition.

Let us, moreover, consent to call a noun or a verb an expression only, and not a proposition, since it is not possible for a man to speak in this way when he is expressing something, in such a way as to make a statement, whether his utterance is an answer to a question or an act of his own initiation.

To return: of propositions one kind is simple, i.e. that which 20 asserts or denies something of something, the other composite, i.e. that which is compounded of simple propositions. A simple proposition is a statement, with meaning, as to the presence of something in a subject or its absence, in the present, past, or future, according to the divisions of time.

An affirmation is a positive assertion of something about 25 something, a denial a negative assertion.

Now it is possible both to affirm and to deny the presence of something which is present or of something which is not, and since these same affirmations and denials are possible with reference to those times which lie outside the present, it would be possible to contradict any affirmation or denial. Thus it is plain 30 that every affirmation has an opposite denial, and similarly every denial an opposite affirmation.

We will call such a pair of propositions a pair of contradictories. Those positive and negative propositions are said to be contradictory which have the same subject and predicate. The identity of subject and of predicate must not be 'equivocal.' In- 35 deed there are definitive qualifications besides this, which we make to meet the casuistries of sophists.

Some things are universal, others individual. By the term 'universal' I mean that which is of such a nature as to be predicated of many subjects, by 'individual' that which is not thus predicated. Thus 'man' is a universal, 'Callias' an individual. 40

Our propositions necessarily sometimes concern a universal 17ᵇ subject, sometimes an individual.

If, then, a man states a positive and a negative proposition of universal character with regard to a universal, these two propositions are 'contrary.' By the expression 'a proposition of universal 5 character with regard to a universal,' such propositions as 'every man is white,' 'no man is white' are meant. When, on the other

hand, the positive and negative propositions, though they have regard to a universal, are yet not of universal character, they will not be contrary, albeit the meaning intended is sometimes contrary. As instances of propositions made with regard to a universal, but not of universal character, we may take the prop-
10 ositions 'man is white,' 'man is not white.' 'Man' is a universal, but the proposition is not made as of universal character; for the word 'every' does not make the subject a universal, but rather gives the proposition a universal character. If, however, both predicate and subject are distributed, the proposition thus constituted is contrary to truth; no affirmation will, under such
15 circumstances, be true. The proposition 'every man is every animal' is an example of this type.

An affirmation is opposed to a denial in the sense which I denote by the term 'contradictory,' when, while the subject remains the same, the affirmation is of universal character and the denial is not. The affirmation 'every man is white' is the *contradictory* of the denial 'not every man is white,' or again, the proposition 'no man is white' is the *contradictory* of the proposition
20 'some men are white.' [2] But propositions are opposed as *contraries* when both the affirmation and the denial are universal, as in the sentences 'every man is white,' 'no man is white,' 'every man is just,' 'no man is just.'

We see that in a pair of this sort both propositions cannot be true, but the contradictories of a pair of contraries can sometimes both be true with reference to the same subject; for in-
25 stance 'not every man is white' and 'some men are white' are both true. Of such corresponding positive and negative propositions as refer to universals and have a universal character, one must be true and the other false. This is the case also when the reference is to individuals, as in the propositions 'Socrates is white,' 'Socrates is not white.'

---

[2]

A contraries E

I   O

	according to the usual logical formula.
Every man is white = A	
No man is white = E	
Some men are white = I	
Not every man is white = O	

When, on the other hand, the reference is to universals, but the propositions are not universal, it is not always the case that 30 one is true and the other false, for it is possible to state truly that man is white and that man is not white and that man is beautiful and that man is not beautiful; for if a man is deformed he is the reverse of beautiful, also if he is progressing towards beauty he is not yet beautiful.

This statement might seem at first sight to carry with it a contradiction, owing to the fact that the proposition 'man is 35 not white' appears to be equivalent to the proposition 'no man is white.' This, however, is not the case, nor are they necessarily at the same time true or false.

It is evident also that the denial corresponding to a single affirmation is itself single; for the denial must deny just that which the affirmation affirms concerning the same subject, and must correspond with the affirmation both in the universal or particular character of the subject and in the distributed 18ᵃ or undistributed sense in which it is understood.

For instance, the affirmation 'Socrates is white' has its proper denial in the proposition 'Socrates is not white.' If anything else be negatively predicated of the subject or if anything else be the subject though the predicate remain the same, the denial will not be the denial proper to that affirmation, but one that is distinct.

The denial proper to the affirmation 'every man is white' is 'not every man is white'; that proper to the affirmation 'some 5 men are white' is 'no man is white,' while that proper to the affirmation 'man is white' is 'man is not white.'

We have shown further that a single denial is contradictorily opposite to a single affirmation and we have explained which these are; we have also stated that contrary are distinct from contradictory propositions and which the contrary are; also that with regard to a pair of opposite propositions it is not always the 10 case that one is true and the other false. We have pointed out, moreover, what the reason of this is and under what circumstances the truth of the one involves the falsity of the other.

*   *   *

In the case of that which is or which has taken place, propositions, whether positive or negative, must be true or false. Again, in the case of a pair of contradictories, either when the subject
30 is universal and the propositions are of a universal character,[3] or when it is individual, as has been said, one of the two must be true and the other false; whereas when the subject is universal, but the propositions are not of a universal character, there is no such necessity. We have discussed this type also in a previous chapter.

When the subject, however, is individual, and that which is predicated of it relates to the future, the case is altered.[4] For if all propositions whether positive or negative are either true or
35 false, then any given predicate must either belong to the subject or not, so that if one man affirms that an event of a given character will take place and another denies it, it is plain that the statement of the one will correspond with reality and that of the other will not. For the predicate cannot both belong and not belong to the subject at one and the same time with regard to the future.

18[b]   Thus, if it is true to say that a thing is white, it must necessarily be white; if the reverse proposition is true, it will of necessity not be white. Again, if it is white, the proposition stating that it is white was true; if it is not white, the proposition to the opposite effect was true. And if it is not white, the man who states that it is is making a false statement; and if the man who states that it is white is making a false statement, it follows that it is not white. It may therefore be argued that it is necessary that affirmations or denials must be either true or false.

5   Now if this be so, nothing is or takes place fortuitously, either in the present or in the future, and there are no real alternatives;

---

[3] Aristotle means that if you start with a universal proposition (A or E) and take the corresponding negation (by which he means O or I), one must be true and the other false.

[4] In this chapter, as Pacius points out, Aristotle deals with four possible theories as to contradictory propositions concerning the future: (1) that both are true; this he refutes, 18[a] 34-9, by implication; (2) that one is true and the other false determinately; this he deals with at length; (3) that both are false; this he dismisses, 18[b] 16-25; (4) that one is true and the other false, indeterminately; this last he commends, 19[a] 23-[b]4.

everything takes place of necessity and is fixed. For either he that affirms that it will take place or he that denies this is in correspondence with fact, whereas if things did not take place of necessity, an event might just as easily not happen as happen; for the meaning of the word 'fortuitous' with regard to present or future events is that reality is so constituted that it may issue in either of two opposite directions.

Again, if a thing is white now, it was true before to say that *10* it would be white, so that of anything that has taken place it was always true to say 'it is' or 'it will be.' But if it was always true to say that a thing is or will be, it is not possible that it should not be or not be about to be, and when a thing cannot not come to be, it is impossible that it should not come to be, and when it is impossible that it should not come to be, it must come to be. All, then, that is about to be must of necessity take *15* place. It results from this that nothing is uncertain or fortuitous, for if it were fortuitous it would not be necessary.

Again, to say that neither the affirmation nor the denial is true, maintaining, let us say, that an event neither will take place nor will not take place, is to take up a position impossible to defend. In the first place, though facts should prove the one proposition false, the opposite would still be untrue.[5] Secondly, *20* if it was true to say that a thing was both white and large, both these qualities must necessarily belong to it; and if they will belong to it the next day they must necessarily belong to it the next day. But if an event is neither to take place nor not to take place the next day, the element of chance will be eliminated.[6] For example, it would be necessary that a sea-fight should neither take place nor fail to take place on the next day.   *25*

These awkward results and others of the same kind follow, if it is an irrefragable law that of every pair of contradictory propositions, whether they have regard to universals and are stated as universally applicable, or whether they have regard to individuals, one must be true and the other false, and that there *30* are no real alternatives, but that all that is or takes place is the

---

[5] *sc. 'ex hypothesi:* and thus the Law of Excluded Middle would be violated.'
[6] *sc.* 'and thus this suggestion does not prove any amendment on the first.'

outcome of necessity. There would be no need to deliberate or
to take trouble, on the supposition that if we should adopt a
certain course, a certain result would follow, while, if we did
not, the result would not follow. For a man may predict an
event ten thousand years beforehand, and another may predict
35 the reverse; that which was truly predicted at the moment in the
past will [7] of necessity take place in the fullness of time.

Further, it makes no difference whether people have or have
not actually made the contradictory statements. For it is manifest that the circumstances are not influenced by the fact of an
affirmation or denial on the part of anyone. For events will not
take place or fail to take place because it was stated that they
would or would not take place, nor is this any more the case if
the prediction dates back ten thousand years or any other space
19ª of time. Wherefore, if through all time the nature of things
was so constituted that a prediction about an event was true,
then through all time it was necessary that that prediction
should find fulfilment; and with regard to all events,[8] circumstances have always been such that their occurrence is a matter
of necessity. For that of which someone has said truly that it
5 will be, cannot fail to take place; and of that which takes place,
it was always true to say that it would be.

Yet this view leads to an impossible conclusion; for we see
that both deliberation and action are causative with regard to
the future, and that, to speak more generally, in those things
10 which are not continuously actual there is a potentiality in
either direction. Such things may either be or not be; events also
therefore may either take place or not take place. There are
many obvious instances of this. It is possible that this coat may
be cut in half, and yet it may not be cut in half, but wear out
15 first. In the same way, it is possible that it should not be cut in
half; unless this were so, it would not be possible that it should
wear out first. So it is therefore with all other events which possess this kind of potentiality. It is therefore plain that it is not of
necessity that everything is or takes place; but in some instances

---

[7] *sc.* 'on our hypothesis.'
[8] *sc.* 'on our hypothesis.'

there are real alternatives, in which case the affirmation is no
more true and no more false than the denial; while some exhibit 20
a predisposition and general tendency in one direction or the
other, and yet can issue in the opposite direction by exception.

Now that which is must needs be when it is, and that which is
not must needs not be when it is not. Yet it cannot be said
without qualification that all existence and non-existence is the
outcome of necessity. For there is a difference between saying 25
that that which is, when it is, must needs be, and simply saying
that all that is must needs be, and similarly in the case of that
which is not. In the case, also, of two contradictory propositions
this holds good. Everything must either be or not be, whether
in the present or in the future, but it is not always possible to
distinguish and state determinately which of these alternatives
must necessarily come about.

Let me illustrate. A sea-fight must either take place to-morrow 30
or not, but it is not necessary that it should take place to-morrow,
neither is it necessary that it should not take place, yet it is
necessary that it either should or should not take place to-
morrow. Since propositions correspond with facts, it is evident
that when in future events there is a real alternative, and a
potentiality in contrary directions, the corresponding affirmation and denial have the same character.

This is the case with regard to that which is not always ex- 35
istent or not always non-existent. One of the two propositions in
such instances must be true and the other false, but we cannot
say determinately that this or that is false, but must leave the
alternative undecided. One may indeed be more likely to be
true than the other, but it cannot be either actually true or
actually false. It is therefore plain that it is not necessary 19ᵇ
that of an affirmation and a denial one should be true and the
other false. For in the case of that which exists potentially, but
not actually, the rule which applies to that which exists actually
does not hold good. The case is rather as we have indicated.

An affirmation is the statement of a fact with regard to a 5
subject, and this subject is either a noun or that which has no
name; the subject and predicate in an affirmation must each

denote a single thing. I have already explained what is meant by
a noun and by that which has no name; for I stated that the expression 'not-man' was not a noun, in the proper sense of the
word, but an indefinite noun, denoting as it does in a certain
sense a single thing. Similarly the expression 'does not enjoy
10 health' is not a verb proper, but an indefinite verb. Every affirmation, then, and every denial, will consist of a noun and a verb,
either definite or indefinite.

There can be no affirmation or denial without a verb; for the
expressions 'is,' 'will be,' 'was,' 'is coming to be,' and the like are
verbs according to our definition, since besides their specific
meaning they convey the notion of time.

Thus the primary affirmation and denial are as follows: 'man
15 is,' 'man is not.' Next to these, there are the propositions: 'not-
man is,' 'not-man is not.' Again we have the propositions: 'every
man is,' 'every man is not,' 'all that is not-man is,' 'all that is not-
man is not.' The same classification holds good with regard to
such periods of time as lie outside the present.

*   *   *

20ª   When the verb 'is' does not fit the structure of the sentence
(for instance, when the verbs 'walks,' 'enjoys health' are used),
that scheme applies, which applied when the word 'is' was
added.

5   Thus we have the propositions: 'every man enjoys health,'
'every man does-not-enjoy-health,' 'all that is not-man enjoys
health,' 'all that is not-man does-not-enjoy-health.'

We must not in these propositions use the expression 'not
every man.' The negative must be attached to the word 'man,'
for the word 'every' does not give to the subject a universal sig-
10 nificance, but implies that, as a subject, it is distributed. This
is plain from the following pairs: 'man enjoys health,' 'man does
not enjoy health'; 'not-man enjoys health,' 'not-man does not
enjoy health.' These propositions differ from the former in being indefinite and not universal in character. Thus the adjec-
tives 'every' and 'no' have no additional significance except that
the subject, whether in a positive or in a negative sentence, is

distributed. The rest of the sentence, therefore, will in each
case be the same.   *15*

Since the contrary of the proposition 'every animal is just' is
'no animal is just,' it is plain that these two propositions will
never both be true at the same time or with reference to the
same subject. Sometimes, however, the contradictories of these
contraries will both be true, as in the instance before us: the
propositions 'not every animal is just' and 'some animals are
just' are both true.

Further, the proposition 'no man is just' follows from the *20*
proposition 'every man is not-just' and the proposition 'not
every man is not-just,' which is the opposite of 'every man is
not-just,' follows from the proposition 'some men are just'; for
if this be true, there must be some just men.

It is evident, also, that when the subject is individual, if a
question is asked and the negative answer is the true one, a
certain positive proposition is also true. Thus, if the question *25*
were asked 'Is Socrates wise?' and the negative answer were the
true one, the positive inference 'Then Socrates is unwise' is correct. But no such inference is correct in the case of universals,
but rather a negative proposition. For instance, if to the question 'Is every man wise?' the answer is 'no,' the inference 'Then
every man is unwise' is false. But under these circumstances the
inference 'Not every man is wise' is correct. This last is the con- *30*
tradictory, the former the contrary. Negative expressions, which
consist of an indefinite noun or predicate, such as 'not-man' or
'not-just,' may seem to be denials containing neither noun nor
verb in the proper sense of the words. But they are not. For a
denial must always be either true or false, and he that uses the *35*
expression 'not-man,' if nothing more be added, is not nearer
but rather further from making a true or a false statement than
he who uses the expression 'man.' [9]

The propositions 'everything that is not man is just,' and the
contradictory of this, are not equivalent to any of the other
propositions; on the other hand, the proposition 'everything

----

[9] Presumably because the indefinite noun has less complete meaning than the
noun proper.

40 that is not man is not just' is equivalent to the proposition 'nothing that is not man is just.'

20ᵇ   The conversion of the position of subject and predicate in a sentence involves no difference in its meaning. Thus we say 'man is white' and 'white is man.' If these were not equivalent, there would be more than one contradictory to the same proposition, whereas it has been demonstrated that each proposition has one proper contradictory and one only. For of the
5 proposition 'man is white' the appropriate contradictory is 'man is not white,' and of the proposition 'white is man,' if its meaning be different, the contradictory will either be 'white is not not-man' or 'white is not man.' Now the former of these is the contradictory of the proposition 'white is not-man,' and the latter of these is the contradictory of the proposition 'man is white';[10] thus there will be two contradictories to one proposition.

10   It is evident, therefore, that the inversion of the relative position of subject and predicate does not affect the sense of affirmations and denials.

*   *   *

PRIOR ANALYTICS

*   *   *

24ᵇ   A syllogism is discourse in which, certain things being stated, something other than what is stated follows of necessity

---

[10] Aristotle really begs the question here, when he states that 'white is not man' is the denial of 'man is white.' Pacius explains that 'man is not white' and 'man is white' are in exactly the same relation each to each as 'white is not man' and 'man is white,' and that therefore 'white is not man' and 'man is not white' are identical. This seems fair, but is in itself sufficient to prove the point at issue at once. The argument of the whole, therefore, is unnecessarily complicated.

from their being so. I mean by the last phrase that they produce 20 the consequence, and by this, that no further term is required from without in order to make the consequence necessary.

I call that a perfect syllogism which needs nothing other than what has been stated to make plain what necessarily follows; a syllogism is imperfect, if it needs either one or more proposi- 25 tions, which are indeed the necessary consequences of the terms set down, but have not been expressly stated as premisses.

That one term should be included in another as in a whole is the same as for the other to be predicated of all of the first. And we say that one term is predicated of all of another, whenever no instance of the subject can be found of which the other term cannot be asserted: 'to be predicated of none' must be 30 understood in the same way.

Every premiss states that something either is or must be or 25ᵃ may be the attribute of something else; of premisses of these three kinds some are affirmative, others negative, in respect of each of the three modes of attribution; again some affirmative and negative premisses are universal, others particular, others 5 indefinite. It is necessary then that in universal attribution the terms of the negative premiss should be convertible, e.g. if no pleasure is good, then no good will be pleasure; the terms of the affirmative must be convertible, not however universally, but in part, e.g. if every pleasure is good, some good must be pleasure; the particular affirmative must convert in part (for if 10 some pleasure is good, then some good will be pleasure); but the particular negative need not convert, for if some animal is not man, it does not follow that some man is not animal.

First then take a universal negative with the terms *A* and *B*. 15 If no *B* is *A*, neither can any *A* be *B*. For if some *A* (say *C*) were *B*, it would not be true that no *B* is *A*; for *C* is a *B*. But if every *B* is *A*, then some *A* is *B*. For if no *A* were *B*, then no *B* could be *A*. But we assumed that every *B* is *A*. Similarly too, if the 20 premiss is particular. For if some *B* is *A*, then some of the *A*s must be *B*. For if none were, then no *B* would be *A*. But if some *B* is not *A*, there is no necessity that some of the *A*s should not

25 be *B*; e.g. let *B* stand for animal and *A* for man. Not every animal is a man; but every man is an animal.

*　　*　　*

25ᵇ   After these distinctions we now state by what means, when,
and how every syllogism is produced; subsequently we must
speak of demonstration. Syllogism should be discussed before
30 demonstration, because syllogism is the more general: the demonstration is a sort of syllogism, but not every syllogism is a
demonstration.

Whenever three terms are so related to one another that the
last is contained in the middle as in a whole, and the middle is
either contained in, or excluded from, the first as in or from a
35 whole, the extremes must be related by a perfect syllogism. I
call that term middle which is itself contained in another and
contains another in itself: in position also this comes in the
middle. By extremes I mean both that term which is itself contained in another and that in which another is contained. If *A*
is predicated of all *B*, and *B* of all *C*, *A* must be predicated of
40 all *C*: we have already explained what we mean by 'predicated
of all.' Similarly also, if *A* is predicated of no *B*, and *B* of
26ᵃ all *C*, it is necessary that no *C* will be *A*.

But if the first term belongs to all the middle, but the middle
to none of the last term, there will be no syllogism in respect
of the extremes; for nothing necessary follows from the terms
being so related; for it is possible that the first should belong
5 either to all or to none of the last, so that neither a particular
nor a universal conclusion is necessary. But if there is no necessary consequence, there cannot be a syllogism by means of these
premisses. As an example of a universal affirmative relation between the extremes we may take the terms animal, man, horse;
of a universal negative relation, the terms animal, man, stone.
10 Nor again can a syllogism be formed when neither the first term
belongs to any of the middle, nor the middle to any of the last.
As an example of a positive relation between the extremes take
the terms science, line, medicine: of a negative relation science,
line, unit.

*   *   *

It is evident also that all the syllogisms in this figure are 26ᵇ
perfect (for they are all completed by means of the premisses 30
originally taken) and that all conclusions are proved by this
figure, viz. universal and particular, affirmative and negative.
Such a figure I call the first.

Whenever the same thing belongs to all of one subject, and
to none of another, or to all of each subject or to none of either, 35
I call such a figure the second; by middle term in it I mean that
which is predicated of both subjects, by extremes the terms of
which this is said, by major extreme that which lies near the
middle, by minor that which is further away from the middle.
The middle term stands outside the extremes, and is first in 27ᵃ
position. A syllogism cannot be perfect anyhow in this figure, but
it may be valid whether the terms are related universally or not.

If then the terms are related universally a syllogism will be
possible, whenever the middle belongs to all of one subject and
to none of another (it does not matter which has the negative 5
relation), but in no other way. Let M be predicated of no N,
but of all O. Since, then, the negative relation is convertible,
N will belong to no M: but M was assumed to belong to all O:
consequently N will belong to no O. This has already been
proved. Again if M belongs to all N, but to no O, then N will 10
belong to no O. For if M belongs to no O, O belongs to no M:
but M (as was said) belongs to all N: O then will belong to no
N: for the first figure has again been formed. But since the
negative relation is convertible, N will belong to no O. Thus
it will be the same syllogism that proves both conclusions.   15

It is possible to prove these results also by reduction *ad impossibile*.

*   *   *

It is clear then from what has been said that if the terms 28ᵃ
are related to one another in the way stated, a syllogism results
of necessity; and if there is a syllogism, the terms must be so
related. But it is evident also that all the syllogisms in this figure

5 are imperfect: for all are made perfect by certain supplementary statements, which either are contained in the terms of necessity or are assumed as hypotheses, i.e. when we prove *per impossibile*. And it is evident that an affirmative conclusion is not attained by means of this figure, but all are negative, whether universal or particular.

10   But if one term belongs to all, and another to none, of a third, or if both belong to all, or to none, of it, I call such a figure the third; by middle term in it I mean that of which both the predicates are predicated, by extremes I mean the predicates, by the major extreme that which is further from the middle, by 15 the minor that which is nearer to it. The middle term stands outside the extremes, and is last in position. A syllogism cannot be perfect in this figure either, but it may be valid whether the terms are related universally or not to the middle term.

*   *   *

It is clear then in this figure also when a syllogism will be possible and when not, if the terms are related universally. For whenever both the terms are affirmative, there will be a syllogism to prove that one extreme belongs to some of the other; but when they are negative, no syllogism will be possible. 28ᵇ But when one is negative, the other affirmative, if the major is negative, the minor affirmative, there will be a syllogism to prove that the one extreme does not belong to some of the other: but if the relation is reversed, no syllogism will be possible.

*   *   *

29ᵃ   It is evident also that in all the figures, whenever a proper 20 syllogism does not result, if both the terms are affirmative or negative nothing necessary follows at all, but if one is affirmative, the other negative, and if the negative is stated universally, a syllogism always results relating the minor[1] to the major term,[2] e.g. if *A* belongs to all or some *B*, and *B* belongs

---

[1] As predicate.
[2] As subject.

to no *C*: for if the premisses are converted it is necessary that 25
C does not belong to some *A*. Similarly also in the other figures:
a syllogism always results by means of conversion. It is evident
also that the substitution of an indefinite for a particular affirmative will effect the same syllogism in all the figures.

It is clear too that all the imperfect syllogisms are made per- 30
fect by means of the first figure. For all are brought to a conclusion either ostensively or *per impossibile*. In both ways the
first figure is formed: if they are made perfect ostensively, because (as we saw) all are brought to a conclusion by means of
conversion, and conversion produces the first figure: if they are 35
proved *per impossibile*, because on the assumption of the false
statement the syllogism comes about by means of the first figure,
e.g. in the last figure, if *A* and *B* belong to all *C*, it follows that
A belongs to some *B*: for if *A* belonged to no *B*, and *B* belongs
to all *C*, *A* would belong to no *C*: but (as we stated) it belongs
to all *C*. Similarly also with the rest.

It is possible also to reduce all syllogisms to the *univer-* 29ᵇ
sal syllogisms in the first figure. Those in the second figure
are clearly made perfect by these, though not all in the same
way; the universal syllogisms are made perfect by converting the
negative premiss, each of the particular syllogisms by reduction 5
ad impossibile. In the first figure particular syllogisms are indeed made perfect by themselves, but it is possible also to prove
them by means of the second figure, reducing them *ad impossibile*, e.g. if *A* belongs to all *B*, and *B* to some *C*, it follows that
A belongs to some *C*. For if it belonged to no *C*, and belongs
to all *B*, then *B* will belong to no *C*: this we know by means 10
of the second figure. Similarly also demonstration will be possible in the case of the negative. For if *A* belongs to no *B*, and
B belongs to some *C*, *A* will not belong to some *C*: for if it belonged to all *C*, and belongs to no *B*, then *B* will belong to no
C: and this (as we saw) is the middle figure. Consequently, since 15
all syllogisms in the middle figure can be reduced to universal
syllogisms in the first figure, and since particular syllogisms in
the first figure can be reduced to syllogisms in the middle figure,
it is clear that particular syllogisms can be reduced to universal

20 syllogisms in the first figure. Syllogisms in the third figure, if the
terms are universal, are directly made perfect by means of those
syllogisms; but, when one of the premisses is particular, by
means of the *particular* syllogisms in the first figure: and these
(we have seen) may be reduced to the universal syllogisms in
the first figure: consequently also the particular syllogisms in
the third figure may be so reduced. It is clear then that all syl-
25 logisms may be reduced to the universal syllogisms in the first
figure.

We have stated then how syllogisms which prove that something belongs or does not belong to something else are constituted, both how syllogisms of the same figure are constituted
in themselves, and how syllogisms of different figures are related
to one another.

*   *   *

POSTERIOR ANALYTICS

89ᵇ   The kinds of question we ask are as many as the kinds
of things which we know. They are in fact four:—(1) whether
the connexion of an attribute with a thing is a fact, (2) what
is the reason of the connexion, (3) whether a thing exists,
25 (4) what is the nature of the thing. Thus, when our question
concerns a complex of thing and attribute and we ask whether
the thing is thus or otherwise qualified—whether, e.g., the sun
suffers eclipse or not—then we are asking as to the fact of a connexion. That our inquiry ceases with the discovery that the sun
does suffer eclipse is an indication of this; and if we know from
the start that the sun suffers eclipse, we do not inquire whether
it does so or not. On the other hand, when we know the fact we
ask the reason; as, for example, when we know that the sun is

being eclipsed and that an earthquake is in progress, it is the *30*
reason of eclipse or earthquake into which we inquire.

Where a complex is concerned, then, those are the two questions we ask; but for some objects of inquiry we have a different
kind of question to ask, such as whether there is or is not a cen-
taur or a God. (By 'is or is not' I mean 'is or is not, without
further qualification'; as opposed to 'is or is not (e.g.) white.')
On the other hand, when we have ascertained the thing's existence, we inquire as to its nature, asking, for instance, 'what,
then, is God?' or 'what is man?'   *35*

These, then, are the four kinds of question we ask, and it is
in the answers to these questions that our knowledge consists.

Now when we ask whether a connexion is a fact, or whether
a thing without qualification *is,* we are really asking whether
the connexion or the thing has a 'middle'; and when we have
ascertained either that the connexion is a fact or that the thing
is—i.e. ascertained either the partial or the unqualified being **90***
of the thing—and are proceeding to ask the reason of the
connexion or the nature of the thing, then we are asking what
the 'middle' is.

(By distinguishing the fact of the connexion and the existence
of the thing as respectively the partial and the unqualified being
of the thing, I mean that if we ask 'does the moon suffer
eclipse?,' or 'does the moon wax?,' the question concerns a part
of the thing's being; for what we are asking in such questions
is whether a thing is this or that, i.e. has or has not this or that
attribute: whereas, if we ask whether the moon or night exists,
the question concerns the unqualified being of a thing.)

We conclude that in all our inquiries we are asking either *5*
whether there is a 'middle' or what the 'middle' is: for the
'middle' here is precisely the cause, and it is the cause that we
seek in all our inquiries. Thus, 'Does the moon suffer eclipse?'
means 'Is there or is there not a cause producing eclipse of the
moon?,' and when we have learnt that there is, our next question is, 'What, then, is this cause?'; for the cause through which
a thing *is*—not *is this or that,* i.e. has this or that attribute, but *10*

without qualification *is*—and the cause through which it is—
not *is* without qualification, but *is this or that* as having some
essential attribute or some accident—are both alike the 'middle.'
By that which *is* without qualification I mean the subject, e.g.
moon or earth or sun or triangle; by that which a subject *is* (in
the partial sense) I mean a property, e.g. eclipse, equality or inequality, interposition or non-interposition. For in all these
examples it is clear that the nature of the thing and the reason
15 of the fact are identical: the question 'What is eclipse?' and its
answer 'The privation of the moon's light by the interposition
of the earth' are identical with the question 'What is the reason
of eclipse?' or 'Why does the moon suffer eclipse?' and the reply
'Because of the failure of light through the earth's shutting it
out.' Again, for 'What is a concord? A commensurate numerical
ratio of a high and a low note,' we may substitute 'What reason
20 makes a high and a low note concordant? Their relation according to a commensurate numerical ratio.' 'Are the high and the
low note concordant?' is equivalent to 'Is their ratio commensurate?'; and when we find that it is commensurate, we ask
'What, then, is their ratio?'

Cases in which the 'middle' is sensible show that the object
25 of our inquiry is always the 'middle': we inquire, because we
have not perceived it, whether there is or is not a 'middle' caus-
ing, e.g. an eclipse. On the other hand, if we were on the moon
we should not be inquiring either as to the fact or the reason,
but both fact and reason would be obvious simultaneously. For
the act of perception would have enabled us to know the universal too; since, the present fact of an eclipse being evident,
perception would then at the same time give us the present fact
30 of the earth's screening the sun's light, and from this would arise
the universal.

Thus, as we maintain, to know a thing's nature is to know
the reason why it is; and this is equally true of things in so
far as they are said without qualification to *be* as opposed to
being possessed of some attribute, and in so far as they are said
to be possessed of some attribute such as equal to two right
angles, or greater or less.

It is clear, then, that all questions are a search for a 'middle.' *35* Let us now state how essential nature is revealed, and in what way it can be reduced to demonstration; what definition is, and what things are definable. And let us first discuss certain difficulties which these questions raise, beginning what we **90ᵇ** have to say with a point most intimately connected with our immediately preceding remarks, namely the doubt that might be felt as to whether or not it is possible to know the same thing in the same relation, both by definition and by demonstration. It might, I mean, be urged that definition is held to concern essential nature and is in every case universal and affirmative; whereas, on the other hand, some conclusions are negative and *5* some are not universal; e.g. all in the second figure are negative, none in the third are universal. And again, not even all affirmative conclusions in the first figure are definable, e.g. 'every triangle has its angles equal to two right angles.' An argument proving this difference between demonstration and definition is that to have scientific knowledge of the demonstrable is identical with possessing a demonstration of it: hence if demonstra- *10* tion of such conclusions as these is possible, there clearly cannot also be definition of them. If there could, one might know such a conclusion also in virtue of its definition without possessing the demonstration of it; for there is nothing to stop our having the one without the other.

Induction too will sufficiently convince us of this difference; for never yet by defining anything—essential attribute or acci- *15* dent—did we get knowledge of it. Again, if to define is to acquire knowledge of a substance, at any rate such attributes are not substances.

It is evident, then, that not everything demonstrable can be defined. What then? Can everything definable be demonstrated, or not? There is one of our previous arguments which covers this too. Of a single thing *qua* single there is a single scientific *20* knowledge. Hence, since to know the demonstrable scientifically is to possess the demonstration of it, an impossible consequence will follow:—possession of its definition without its demonstration will give knowledge of the demonstrable.

Moreover, the basic premisses of demonstrations are definitions, and it has already been shown that these will be found
25 indemonstrable; either the basic premisses will be demonstrable
and will depend on prior premisses, and the regress will be endless; or the primary truths will be indemonstrable definitions.

But if the definable and the demonstrable are not wholly the
same, may they yet be partially the same? Or is that impossible,
because there can be no demonstration of the definable? There
30 can be none, because definition is of the essential nature or being of something, and all demonstrations evidently posit and
assume the essential nature—mathematical demonstrations, for
example, the nature of unity and the odd, and all the other sciences likewise. Moreover, every demonstration proves a predicate of a subject as attaching or as not attaching to it, but in
35 definition one thing is not predicated of another; we do not,
e.g., predicate animal of biped nor biped of animal, nor yet
figure of plane—plane not being figure nor figure plane. Again,
to prove essential nature is not the same as to prove the
91ᵃ fact of a connexion. Now definition reveals essential nature,
demonstration reveals that a given attribute attaches or does
not attach to a given subject; but different things require different demonstrations[1]—unless the one demonstration is related to
the other as part to whole. I add this because if all triangles have
been proved to possess angles equal to two right angles, then
this attribute has been proved to attach to isosceles; for isosceles
5 is a part of which all triangles constitute the whole. But in the
case before us the fact and the essential nature are not so related to one another, since the one is not a part of the other.

So it emerges that not all the definable is demonstrable nor
all the demonstrable definable; and we may draw the general
conclusion that there is no identical object of which it is possi-
10 ble to possess both a definition and a demonstration. It follows
obviously that definition and demonstration are neither identical nor contained either within the other: if they were, their
objects would be related either as identical or as whole and part.

---

[1] Aristotle argues that what definition reveals and what ordinary demonstration reveals are different. Therefore if definition is a kind of demonstration it
is at any rate not the ordinary kind, and the 'definable' has not been shown to
be the 'demonstrable' in the sense required.

*   *   *

We must now start afresh and consider which of these con- 93ᵃ
clusions are sound and which are not, and what is the nature
of definition, and whether essential nature is in any sense demonstrable and definable or in none.

Now to know its essential nature is, as we said, the same as
to know the cause of a thing's existence, and the proof of this
depends on the fact that a thing must have a cause. Moreover, 5
this cause is either identical with the essential nature of the
thing or distinct from it;² and if its cause is distinct from it, the
essential nature of the thing is either demonstrable or indemonstrable. Consequently, if the cause is distinct from the thing's
essential nature and demonstration is possible, the cause must
be the middle term, and, the conclusion proved being universal
and affirmative, the proof is in the first figure. So the method
just examined of proving it through another essential nature
would be one way of proving essential nature, because a con- 10
clusion containing essential nature must be inferred through a
middle which is an essential nature just as a 'peculiar' property
must be inferred through a middle which is a 'peculiar' property; so that of the two definable natures of a single thing this
method will prove one and not the other.³

Now it was said before that this method could not amount
to demonstration of essential nature—it is actually a dialectical 15
proof of it—so let us begin again and explain by what method
it can be demonstrated. When we are aware of a fact we seek
its reason, and though sometimes the fact and the reason dawn
on us simultaneously, yet we cannot apprehend the reason a moment sooner than the fact; and clearly in just the same way we
cannot apprehend a thing's definable form without apprehend-

---

² 'distinct from it'; i.e. in the case of *properties*, with the definition of which
Aristotle is alone concerned in this chapter. The being of a property consists in
its inherence in a substance through a middle which defines it.

³ Aristotle speaks of two moments of the definable form as two essential natures. His argument amounts to this: that if the conclusion contains the whole
definition, the question has been begged in the premisses. Hence syllogism—and
even so merely dialectical syllogism—is only possible if premisses and conclusion
each contain a part of the definition.

20 ing that it exists, since while we are ignorant whether it exists
we cannot know its essential nature. Moreover we are aware
whether a thing exists or not sometimes through apprehending
an element in its character, and sometimes accidentally,[4] as, for
example, when we are aware of thunder as a noise in the clouds,
of eclipse as a privation of light, or of man as some species of
animal, or of the soul as a self-moving thing. As often as we
25 have accidental knowledge that the thing exists, we must be in
a wholly negative state as regards awareness of its essential nature; for we have not got genuine knowledge even of its existence, and to search for a thing's essential nature when we are
unaware that it exists is to search for nothing. On the other
hand, whenever we apprehend an element in the thing's character there is less difficulty. Thus it follows that the degree of
our knowledge of a thing's essential nature is determined by
the sense in which we are aware that it exists. Let us then take
30 the following as our first instance of being aware of an element
in the essential nature. Let A be eclipse, C the moon, B the
earth's acting as a screen. Now to ask whether the moon is
eclipsed or not is to ask whether or not B has occurred. But that
is precisely the same as asking whether A has a defining condition; and if this condition actually exists, we assert that A also
actually exists. Or again we may ask which side of a contradiction the defining condition necessitates: does it make the angles
of a triangle equal or not equal to two right angles? When we
35 have found the answer, if the premisses are immediate, we know
fact and reason together; if they are not immediate, we know
the fact without the reason, as in the following example: let C
be the moon, A eclipse, B the fact that the moon fails to produce shadows[5] though she is full and though no visible body
intervenes between us and her. Then if B, failure to produce
93ᵇ shadows in spite of the absence of an intervening body, is
attributable to C, and A, eclipse, is attributable to B, it is clear
that the moon is eclipsed, but the reason why is not yet clear,

---

[4] The distinction is that between genuine knowledge of a connexion through
its cause and accidental knowledge of it through a middle not the cause.

[5] i.e. that there is no moonlight casting shadows on the earth on a clear night
at full moon.

and we know that eclipse exists, but we do not know what its essential nature is. But when it is clear that *A* is attributable to *C* and we proceed to ask the reason of this fact, we are inquiring 5 what is the nature of *B*: is it the earth's acting as a screen, or the moon's rotation or her extinction? But *B* is the definition of the other term, viz., in these examples, of the major term *A*; for eclipse is constituted by the earth acting as a screen. Thus, ⟨1⟩ 'What is thunder?' 'The quenching of fire in cloud,' and (2) 'Why does it thunder?' 'Because fire is quenched in the cloud,' are equivalent. Let *C* be cloud, *A* thunder, *B* the quenching of 10 fire. Then *B* is attributable to *C*, cloud, since fire is quenched in it; and *A*, noise, is attributable to *B*; and *B* is assuredly the definition of the major term *A*. If there be a further mediating cause of *B*, it will be one of the remaining partial definitions of *A*.

We have stated then how essential nature is discovered and 15 becomes known, and we see that, while there is no syllogism— i.e. no demonstrative syllogism—of essential nature, yet it is through syllogism, viz. demonstrative syllogism, that essential nature is exhibited. So we conclude that neither can the essential nature of anything which has a cause distinct from itself be known without demonstration, nor can it be demonstrated; and this is what we contended in our preliminary discussions. 20

Now while some things have a cause distinct from themselves, others have not. Hence it is evident that there are essential natures which are immediate, that is are basic premisses; and of these not only *that* they are but also *what* they are must be assumed or revealed in some other way. This too is the actual procedure of the arithmetician, who assumes both the nature 25 and the existence of unit. On the other hand, it is possible (in the manner explained) to exhibit through demonstration the essential nature of things which have a 'middle,' i.e. a cause of their substantial being other than that being itself; but we do not thereby demonstrate it.

Since definition is said to be the statement of a thing's nature, obviously one kind of definition will be a statement of the 30 meaning of the name, or of an equivalent nominal formula. A

definition in this sense tells you, e.g., the meaning of the phrase
'triangular character.' When we are aware that triangle exists,
we inquire the reason why it exists. But it is difficult thus to
learn the definition of things the existence of which we do not
genuinely know—the cause of this difficulty being, as we said
35 before, that we only know accidentally whether or not the thing
exists. Moreover, a statement may be a unity in either of two
ways, by conjunction, like the *Iliad,* or because it exhibits a
single predicate as inhering not accidentally in a single subject.[6]

That then is one way of defining definition. Another kind of
definition is a formula exhibiting the cause of a thing's exist-
94ª ence. Thus the former signifies without proving, but the
latter will clearly be a *quasi*-demonstration of essential nature,
differing from demonstration in the arrangement of its terms.
For there is a difference between stating why it thunders, and
stating what is the essential nature of thunder; since the first
statement will be 'Because fire is quenched in the clouds,' while
the statement of what the nature of thunder is will be 'The
5 noise of fire being quenched in the clouds.' Thus the same statement takes a different form: in one form it is continuous[7] demonstration, in the other definition. Again, thunder can be defined as noise in the clouds, which is the conclusion of the
demonstration embodying essential nature. On the other hand
the definition of immediates is an indemonstrable positing of
10 essential nature.

We conclude then that definition is (*a*) an indemonstrable
statement of essential nature, or (*b*) a syllogism of essential nature differing from demonstration in grammatical form, or (*c*)
the conclusion of a demonstration giving essential nature.

Our discussion has therefore made plain (1) in what sense and
15 of what things the essential nature is demonstrable, and in what

---

[6] Presumably a reason for there being a kind of definition other than nominal.
The reference is obviously to 92ᵇ 32.

[7] Demonstration, like a line, is continuous because its premisses are parts which
are conterminous (as linked by middle terms), and there is a movement from
premisses to conclusion. Definition resembles rather the indivisible simplicity of
a point.

sense and of what things it is not; (2) what are the various meanings of the term definition, and in what sense and of what things it proves the essential nature, and in what sense and of what things it does not; (3) what is the relation of definition to demonstration, and how far the same thing is both definable and demonstrable and how far it is not.

We think we have scientific knowledge when we know the *20* cause, and there are four causes: (1) the definable form, (2) an antecedent which necessitates a consequent,[8] (3) the efficient cause, (4) the final cause. Hence each of these can be the middle term of a proof, for[9] (*a*) though the inference from antecedent to necessary consequent does not hold if only one premiss is *25* assumed—two is the minimum—still when there are two it holds on condition that they have a single common middle term. So it is from the assumption of this single middle term that the conclusion follows necessarily. The following example will also show this.[10] Why is the angle in a semicircle a right angle?—or from what assumption does it follow that it is a right angle? Thus, let A be right angle, B the half of two right angles, C the angle in a semicircle. Then B is the cause in virtue of which A, *30* right angle, is attributable to C, the angle in a semicircle, since $B = A$ and the other, viz. C, $= B$, for C is half of two right angles. Therefore it *is* the assumption of B, the half of two right angles, from which it follows that A is attributable to C, i.e. that the angle in a semicircle is a right angle. Moreover, B is

---

[8] By this Aristotle appears to mean the material cause; cf. *Physics* ii, 195ᵃ 18, 19, where the premisses of a syllogism are said to be the material cause of the conclusion. In this chapter Aristotle gives no separate example of formal cause as the middle term of demonstration, and seems rather, in virtue of a different classification of cause, to regard the middle of demonstration as *always* a formal cause because it defines the major term, and as generically embracing material, efficient, and final causes. But as the transition is neither explicit nor complete, this is confusing. In the *Metaphysics* Aristotle teaches that formal, final, and efficient causes coalesce (cf. e.g. *Met.* 1044ᵇ 1, 1070ᵇ 26), while the material cause remains distinct. The treatment of causation here is presumably earlier than the teaching of the *Metaphysics,* though in the last part of the chapter Aristotle is moving towards the position he there adopts.

[9] *sc.* 'lest you should suppose that (2) could not be a middle.'

[10] *sc.* 'that (2) can appear as a middle.'

35 identical with (*b*) the defining form of *A*, since it is what *A*'s
definition[11] signifies. Moreover, the formal cause has already
been shown to be the middle.[12] (*c*) 'Why did the Athenians become involved in the Persian war?' means 'What cause originated the waging of war against the Athenians?' and the answer
*94*ᵇ is, 'Because they raided Sardis with the Eretrians,' since this
originated the war. Let *A* be war, *B* unprovoked raiding, *C*
the Athenians. Then *B*, unprovoked raiding, is true of *C*, the
5 Athenians, and *A* is true of *B*, since men make war on the
unjust aggressor. So *A*, having war waged upon them, is true of
B, the initial aggressors, and *B* is true of *C*, the Athenians, who
were the aggressors. Hence here too the cause—in this case the
efficient cause—is the middle term. (*d*) This is no less true
where the cause is the final cause. E.g. why does one take a walk
after supper? For the sake of one's health. Why does a house
10 exist? For the preservation of one's goods. The end in view is
in the one case health, in the other preservation. To ask the
reason why one must walk after supper is precisely to ask to
what end one must do it. Let *C* be walking after supper, *B* the
non-regurgitation of food, *A* health. Then let walking after
15 supper possess the property of preventing food from rising to
the orifice of the stomach, and let this condition be healthy;
since it seems that *B*, the non-regurgitation of food, is attributable to *C*, taking a walk, and that *A*, health, is attributable to *B*.
What, then, is the cause through which *A*, the final cause, inheres in *C*? It is *B*, the non-regurgitation of food; but *B* is a kind
20 of definition of *A*, for *A* will be explained by it. Why is *B* the
cause of *A*'s belonging to *C*? Because to be in a condition such
as *B* is to be in health. The definitions must be transposed, and
then the detail will become clearer.[13] . . .

---

[11] Cf. Euclid, *Elem.* i, Def. x, but Aristotle may be referring to some earlier
definition. The proof here given that the angle in a semicircle is a right angle
is not that of Euclid iii. 31.
[12] The reference is to 93ᵃ 3 ff., and other passages such as 94ᵃ 5 ff., where the
middle is shown to define the major.
[13] The argument from 94ᵇ 8 is roughly as follows:—
  Health *A*, digestion *B*, walking *C*.
The final cause *A* inheres in *C* through the efficient cause *B*. (*A-B, B-C,* ∴ *A-C*.)

TOPICS

Our treatise proposes to find a line of inquiry where- **100ᵃ**
by we shall be able to reason from opinions that are generally accepted about every problem propounded to us, and *20*
also shall ourselves, when standing up to an argument, avoid
saying anything that will obstruct us. First, then, we must say
what reasoning is, and what its varieties are, in order to grasp
dialectical reasoning: for this is the object of our search in the
treatise before us.

Now reasoning is an argument in which, certain things being *25*
laid down, something other than these necessarily comes about
through them. (*a*) It is a 'demonstration,' when the premisses
from which the reasoning starts are true and primary, or are
such that our knowledge of them has originally come through
premisses which are primary and true: (*b*) reasoning, on the *30*
other hand, is 'dialectical,' if it reasons from opinions that are
generally accepted. Things are 'true' and 'primary' which are
believed on the strength not of anything else but of them- **100ᵇ**
selves: for in regard to the first principles of science it is im-
proper to ask any further for the why and wherefore of them; *20*
each of the first principles should command belief in and by
itself. On the other hand, those opinions are 'generally accepted'
which are accepted by every one, or by the majority or by the
philosophers—i.e. by all, or by the majority, or by the most

⟨But the final cause naturally appears as the effect of the efficient cause; which
means that⟩ *B*, the efficient cause, is a kind of definition of *A*, the final cause.

⟨Since *A* is *B*'s final cause, just as much as *B* is *A*'s efficient cause, *A* is also a
kind of definition of *B*. Hence⟩ we can transpose *A* and *B*, and prove the inherence of *B* in *C* through *A*. (*B-A, A-C, ∴ B-C*.)

This seems to foreshadow the doctrine of the ultimate identity of final, efficient, and formal cause, cf. note on 94ᵃ 22.

notable and illustrious of them. Again (*c*), reasoning is 'contentious' if it starts from opinions that seem to be generally ac-
25 cepted, but are not really such, or again if it merely seems to
reason from opinions that are or seem to be generally accepted.
For not every opinion that seems to be generally accepted actually is generally accepted. For in none of the opinions which
we call generally accepted is the illusion entirely on the surface,
as happens in the case of the principles of contentious argu-
30 ments; for the nature of the fallacy in these is obvious immediately, and as a rule even to persons with little power of
101ª comprehension. So then, of the contentious reasonings mentioned, the former really deserves to be called 'reasoning' as
well, but the other should be called 'contentious reasoning,' but
not 'reasoning,' since it appears to reason, but does not really
do so.

                    *   *   *

25   Next in order after the foregoing, we must say for how many
and for what purposes the treatise is useful. They are three—
intellectual training, casual encounters, and the philosophical
sciences. That it is useful as a training is obvious on the face
of it. The possession of a plan of inquiry will enable us more
30 easily to argue about the subject proposed. For purposes of
casual encounters, it is useful because when we have counted
up the opinions held by most people, we shall meet them on
the ground not of other people's convictions but of their own,
while we shift the ground of any argument that they appear to
us to state unsoundly. For the study of the philosophical sci-
35 ences it is useful, because the ability to raise searching difficulties on both sides of a subject will make us detect more easily
the truth and error about the several points that arise. It has a
further use in relation to the ultimate bases of the principles
used in the several sciences. For it is impossible to discuss them
at all from the principles proper to the particular science in
hand, seeing that the principles are the *prius* of everything else:
101ᵇ it is through the opinions generally held on the particular

points that these have to be discussed, and this task belongs
properly, or most appropriately, to dialectic: for dialectic is a
process of criticism wherein lies the path to the principles of all
inquiries.

*   *   *

First, then, we must see of what parts our inquiry consists.
Now if we were to grasp (a) with reference to how many, and
what kind of, things arguments take place, and with what materials they start, and (b) how we are to become well supplied
with these, we should have sufficiently won our goal. Now the
materials with which arguments start are equal in number, and
are identical, with the subjects on which reasonings take place. *15*
For arguments start with 'propositions,' while the subjects on
which reasonings take place are 'problems.' Now every proposition and every problem indicates either a genus or a peculiarity
or an accident—for the differentia too, applying as it does to a
class (or genus), should be ranked together with the genus.
Since, however, of what is peculiar to anything part signifies
its essence, while part does not, let us divide the 'peculiar' into *20*
both the aforesaid parts, and call that part which indicates the
essence a 'definition,' while of the remainder let us adopt the
terminology which is generally current about these things, and
speak of it as a 'property.' What we have said, then, makes it
clear that according to our present division, the elements turn
out to be four, all told, namely either property or definition or *25*
genus or accident. Do not let any one suppose us to mean that
each of these enunciated by itself constitutes a proposition or
problem, but only that it is from these that both problems and
propositions are formed. The difference between a problem and
a proposition is a difference in the turn of the phrase. For if it *30*
be put in this way, ' " An animal that walks on two feet" is the
definition of man, is it not?' or ' " Animal" is the genus of man,
is it not?' the result is a proposition: but if thus, 'Is "an animal
that walks on two feet" a definition of man or no?' [or 'Is "animal" his genus or no?'] the result is a problem. Similarly too

35 in other cases. Naturally, then, problems and propositions are
equal in number: for out of every proposition you will make a
problem if you change the turn of the phrase.

We must now say what are 'definition,' 'property,' 'genus,'
and 'accident.' A 'definition' is a phrase signifying a thing's es-
102ª sence. It is rendered in the form either of a phrase in lieu of
a term, or of a phrase in lieu of another phrase; for it is sometimes possible to define the meaning of a phrase as well. People
whose rendering consists of a term only, try it as they may,
clearly do not render the definition of the thing in question,
5 because a definition is always a phrase of a certain kind. One
may, however, use the word 'definitory' also of such a remark
as 'The "becoming" is "beautiful," ' and likewise also of the
question, 'Are sensation and knowledge the same or different?'
for argument about definitions is mostly concerned with questions of sameness and difference. In a word we may call 'defini-
10 tory' everything that falls under the same branch of inquiry as
definitions; and that all the above-mentioned examples are of
this character is clear on the face of them. For if we are able to
argue that two things are the same or are different, we shall be
well supplied by the same turn of argument with lines of attack
upon their definitions as well: for when we have shown that
they are not the same we shall have demolished the definition.
15 Observe, please, that the converse of this last statement does
not hold: for to show that they are the same is not enough to
establish a definition. To show, however, that they are not the
same is enough of itself to overthrow it.

A 'property' is a predicate which does not indicate the essence
of a thing, but yet belongs to that thing alone, and is predicated
20 convertibly of it. Thus it is a property of man to be capable of
learning grammar: for if A be a man, then he is capable of
learning grammar, and if he be capable of learning grammar,
he is a man. For no one calls anything a 'property' which may
possibly belong to something else, e.g. 'sleep' in the case of man,
even though at a certain time it may happen to belong to him
25 alone. That is to say, if any such thing were actually to be called
a property, it will be called not a 'property' absolutely, but a

'temporary' or a 'relative' property: for 'being on the right hand side' is a temporary property, while 'two-footed' is in point of fact ascribed as a property in certain relations; e.g. it is a property of man relatively to a horse and a dog. That nothing which may belong to anything else than A is a convertible predicate of A is clear: for it does not necessarily follow that if something *30* is asleep it is a man.

A 'genus' is what is predicated in the category of essence of a number of things exhibiting differences in kind. We should treat as predicates in the category of essence all such things as it would be appropriate to mention in reply to the question, 'What is the object before you?'; as, for example, in the case of *35* man, if asked that question, it is appropriate to say 'He is an animal.' The question, 'Is one thing in the same genus as another or in a different one?' is also a 'generic' question; for a question of that kind as well falls under the same branch of inquiry as the genus: for having argued that 'animal' is the genus of man, and likewise also of ox, we shall have argued that they are in the same genus; whereas if we show that it is the **102ᵇ** genus of the one but not of the other, we shall have argued that these things are not in the same genus.

An 'accident' is (1) something which, though it is none of the foregoing—i.e. neither a definition nor a property nor a genus *5* —yet belongs to the thing: (2) something which may possibly either belong or not belong to any one and the self-same thing, as (e.g.) the 'sitting posture' may belong or not belong to some self-same thing. Likewise also 'whiteness,' for there is nothing to prevent the same thing being at one time white, and at another not white. Of the definitions of accident the second is the *10* better: for if he adopts the first, any one is bound, if he is to understand it, to know already what 'definition' and 'genus' and 'property' are, whereas the second is sufficient of itself to tell us the essential meaning of the term in question. To Accident are to be attached also all comparisons of things together, when *15* expressed in language that is drawn in any kind of way from what happens (*accidit*) to be true of them; such as, for example, the question, 'Is the honourable or the expedient preferable?'

and 'Is the life of virtue or the life of self-indulgence the pleas-
anter?' and any other problem which may happen to be phrased
in terms like these. For in all such cases the question is 'to which
20 of the two does the predicate in question happen (*accidit*) to
belong more closely?' It is clear on the face of it that there is
nothing to prevent an accident from becoming a temporary or
a relative property. Thus the sitting posture is an accident, but
will be a temporary property, whenever a man is the only person sitting, while if he be not the only one sitting, it is still a
25 property relatively to those who are not sitting. So then, there
is nothing to prevent an accident from becoming both a relative
and a temporary property; but a property absolutely it will
never be.

We must not fail to observe that all remarks made in criticism
of a 'property' and 'genus' and 'accident' will be applicable to
'definitions' as well. For when we have shown that the attribute
30 in question fails to belong only to the term defined, as we do
also in the case of a property, or that the genus rendered in the
definition is not the true genus, or that any of the things mentioned in the phrase used does not belong, as would be remarked also in the case of an accident, we shall have demolished
the definition; so that, to use the phrase previously employed,
35 all the points we have enumerated might in a certain sense be
called 'definitory.' But we must not on this account expect to
find a single line of inquiry which will apply universally to
them all: for this is not an easy thing to find, and, even were
one found, it would be very obscure indeed, and of little service
for the treatise before us. Rather, a special plan of inquiry must
be laid down for each of the classes we have distinguished, and
then, starting from the rules that are appropriate in each case,
103ᵃ it will probably be easier to make our way right through the
task before us. So then, as was said before, we must outline
a division of our subject, and other questions we must rele-
gate each to the particular branch to which it most naturally
belongs, speaking of them as 'definitory' and 'generic' questions.
5 The questions I mean have practically been already assigned to
their several branches.

*   *   *

Now one way to confirm that the elements mentioned above **103ᵇ**
are those out of which and through which and to which arguments proceed, is by induction: for if any one were to survey propositions and problems one by one, it would be seen 5
that each was formed either from the definition of something
or from its property or from its genus or from its accident. Another way to confirm it is through reasoning. For every predicate of a subject must of necessity be either convertible with
its subject or not: and if it is convertible, it would be its definition or property, for if it signifies the essence, it is the definition; 10
if not, it is a property: for this was what a property is, viz. what
is predicated convertibly, but does not signify the essence. If,
on the other hand, it is not predicated convertibly of the thing,
it either is or is not one of the terms contained in the definition
of the subject: and if it be one of those terms, then it will be 15
the genus or the differentia, inasmuch as the definition consists
of genus and differentiae; whereas, if it be not one of those
terms, clearly it would be an accident, for accident was said to
be what belongs as an attribute to a subject without being either
its definition or its genus or a property.

Next, then, we must distinguish between the classes of predi- 20
cates in which the four orders in question are found. These are
ten in number: Essence, Quantity, Quality, Relation, Place,
Time, Position, State, Activity, Passivity. For the accident and
genus and property and definition of anything will always be 25
in one of these categories: for all the propositions found through
these signify either something's essence or its quality or quantity or some one of the other types of predicate. It is clear, too,
on the face of it that the man who signifies something's essence
signifies sometimes a substance, sometimes a quality, sometimes
some one of the other types of predicate. For when a man is set 30
before him and he says that what is set there is 'a man' or 'an
animal,' he states its essence and signifies a substance; but when
a white colour is set before him and he says that what is set
there is 'white' or is 'a colour,' he states its essence and signifies

a quality. Likewise, also, if a magnitude of a cubit be set before
him and he says that what is set there is a magnitude of a cubit,
35 he will be describing its essence and signifying a quantity. Likewise, also, in the other cases: for each of these kinds of predicate, if either it be asserted of itself, or its genus be asserted of
it, signifies an essence: if, on the other hand, one kind of predicate is asserted of another kind, it does not signify an essence,
but a quantity or a quality or one of the other kinds of predicate. Such, then, and so many, are the subjects on which argu-
104ª ments take place, and the materials with which they start. How
we are to acquire them, and by what means we are to become
well supplied with them, falls next to be told.

*   *   *

Sophistical Refutations

Let us now discuss sophistic refutations, i.e. what ap-
164ª pear to be refutations but are really fallacies instead. We will
begin in the natural order with the first.

That some reasonings are genuine, while others seem to be
25 so but are not, is evident. This happens with arguments, as also
elsewhere, through a certain likeness between the genuine and
the sham. For physically some people are in a vigorous condi-
20 tion, while others merely seem to be so by [164ᵇ] blowing and
rigging themselves out as the tribesmen do their victims for
sacrifice; and some people are beautiful thanks to their beauty,
while others seem to be so, by dint of embellishing themselves.
So it is, too, with inanimate things; for of these, too, some are
really silver and others gold, while others are not and merely
seem to be such to our sense; e.g. things made of litharge and
25 tin seem to be of silver, while those made of yellow metal look

golden. In the same way both reasoning and refutation are sometimes genuine, sometimes not, though inexperience may make them appear so: for inexperienced people obtain only, as it were, a distant view of these things. For reasoning rests on certain statements such that they involve necessarily the **165ᵃ** assertion of something other than what has been stated, through what has been stated: refutation is reasoning involving the contradictory of the given conclusion. Now some of them do not really achieve this, though they seem to do so for a number of reasons. . . .

         *   *   *

Clearly, then, there exists a class of arguments of this kind, and it is at this kind of ability that those aim whom we call sophists. Let us now go on to discuss how many kinds there are of sophistical arguments, and how many in number are the ele- 35 ments of which this faculty is composed, and how many branches there happen to be of this inquiry, and the other factors that contribute to this art.

Of arguments in dialogue form there are four classes: Didactic, Dialectical, Examination-arguments, and Contentious arguments. Didactic arguments are those that reason **165ᵇ** from the principles appropriate to each subject and not from the opinions held by the answerer (for the learner should take things on trust): dialectical arguments are those that reason from premisses generally accepted, to the contradictory of a given thesis: examination-arguments are those that reason 5 from premisses which are accepted by the answerer and which any one who pretends to possess knowledge of the subject is bound to know—in what manner, has been defined in another treatise: contentious arguments are those that reason or appear to reason to a conclusion from premisses that appear to be generally accepted but are not so. The subject, then, of demonstrative arguments has been discussed in the *Analytics,* while that of dialectic arguments and examination-arguments has been dis- *10* cussed elsewhere: let us now proceed to speak of the arguments used in competitions and contests.

First we must grasp the number of aims entertained by those who argue as competitors and rivals to the death. These are five
15 in number, refutation, fallacy, paradox, solecism, and fifthly to reduce the opponent in the discussion to babbling—i.e. to constrain him to repeat himself a number of times: or it is to produce the appearance of each of these things without the reality. For they choose if possible plainly to refute the other party, or as the second best to show that he is committing some fallacy, or as a third best to lead him into paradox, or fourthly to reduce
20 him to solecism, i.e. to make the answerer, in consequence of the argument, to use an ungrammatical expression; or, as a last resort, to make him repeat himself.

There are two styles of refutation: for some depend on the language used, while some are independent of language. Those
25 ways of producing the false appearance of an argument which depend on language are six in number: they are ambiguity, amphiboly, combination, division of words, accent, form of expression. Of this we may assure ourselves both by induction, and by syllogistic proof based on this—and it may be on other assumptions as well—that this is the number of ways in which we might fail to mean the same thing by the same names or
30 expressions. Arguments such as the following depend upon ambiguity. '. . . Evils are good: for what needs to be is good,
35 and evils must needs be.' For 'what needs to be' has a double meaning: it means what is inevitable, as often is the case with evils, too (for evil of some kind is inevitable), while on the other hand we say of good things as well that they 'need to be.' Moreover, 'The same man is both seated and standing and he is both sick and in health: for it is he who stood up who is stand-
166ª ing, and he who is recovering who is in health: but it is the seated man who stood up, and the sick man who was recovering.' For 'The sick man does so and so,' or 'has so and so done to him' is not single in meaning: sometimes it means 'the man who is sick or is seated now,' sometimes 'the man who was sick formerly.' Of course, the man who was recovering was the sick
5 man, who really was sick at the time: but the man who is in health is not sick at the same time: he is 'the sick man' in the

sense not that he is sick now, but that he was sick formerly. Examples such as the following depend upon amphiboly: 'I wish that you the enemy may capture.' Also the thesis, 'There must be knowledge of what one knows': for it is possible by this phrase to mean that knowledge belongs to both the knower and the known. Also, 'There must be sight of what one sees: one sees the pillar: *ergo* the pillar has sight.' Also, 'What you profess *10* to-be, that you profess-to-be: you profess a stone to-be: *ergo* you profess-to-be a stone.'

*   *   *

Amphiboly and ambiguity, then, depend on these modes of speech. Upon the combination of words there depend instances such as the following: 'A man can walk while sitting, and can write while not writing.' For the meaning is not the same if one *25* divides the words and if one combines them in saying that 'it is possible to walk-while-sitting' [and write while not writing]. The same applies to the latter phrase, too, if one combines the words 'to write-while-not-writing': for then it means that he has the power to write and not to write at once; whereas if one does not combine them, it means that when he is not writing he has *30* the power to write. Also, 'He knows now if he has learnt his letters.' Moreover, there is the saying that 'One single thing if you can carry a crowd you can carry too.'

Upon division depend the propositions that 5 is 2 and 3, and even and odd, and that the greater is equal: for it is that amount and more besides. For the same phrase would not be thought *35* always to have the same meaning when divided and when combined, e.g. 'I made thee a slave once a free man,' and 'God-like Achilles left fifty a hundred men.'

An argument depending upon accent it is not easy to construct in unwritten discussion; in written discussions and in **166**^b poetry it is easier. . . . In the passage about Agamemnon's dream, they say that Zeus did not himself say 'We grant him the fulfilment of his prayer,' but that he bade the dream grant it. Instances such as these, then, turn upon the accentuation.

Others come about owing to the form of expression used, *10*

when what is really different is expressed in the same form. . . .
Thus (e.g.) 'flourishing' is a word which in the form of its expression is like 'cutting' or 'building': yet the one denotes a
certain quality—i.e. a certain condition—while the other denotes a certain action. In the same manner also in the other instances.

20   Refutations, then, that depend upon language are drawn from
these common-place rules. Of fallacies, on the other hand, that
are independent of language there are seven kinds:

(1) that which depends upon Accident:
(2) the use of an expression absolutely or not absolutely but
with some qualification of respect, or place, or time, or relation:
(3) that which depends upon ignorance of what 'refutation'
is:
25   (4) that which depends upon the consequent:
(5) that which depends upon assuming the original conclusion:
(6) stating as cause what is not the cause:
(7) the making of more than one question into one.

Fallacies, then, that depend on Accident occur whenever any
30 attribute is claimed to belong in a like manner to a thing and
to its accident. For since the same thing has many accidents there
is no necessity that all the same attributes should belong to all
of a thing's predicates and to their subject as well. Thus (e.g.), 'If
Coriscus be different from "man," he is different from himself:
for he is a man': or 'If he be different from Socrates, and Socrates
35 be a man, then,' they say, 'he has admitted that Coriscus is different from a man, because it so happens (*accidit*) that the person
from whom he said that he (Coriscus) is different is a man.'

Those that depend on whether an expression is used absolutely or in a certain respect and not strictly, occur whenever
an expression used in a particular sense is taken as though it
167ᵃ were used absolutely, e.g. in the argument 'If what is not is
the object of an opinion, then what is not is': for it is not the
same thing 'to be *x*' and 'to be' absolutely. Or again, 'What is,
is not, if it is not a particular kind of being, e.g. if it is not a

man.' For it is not the same thing 'not to be *x*' and 'not to be' at all: it looks as if it were, because of the closeness of the expres- 5 sion, i.e. because 'to be *x*' is but little different from 'to be,' and 'not to be *x*' from 'not to be.' Likewise also with any argument that turns upon the point whether an expression is used in a certain respect or used absolutely. Thus e.g. 'Suppose an Indian to be black all over, but white in respect of his teeth; then he is both white and not white.'

*   *   *

Other fallacies occur because the terms 'proof' or 'refutation' have not been defined, and because something is left out in their definition. For to refute is to contradict one and the same attribute—not merely the name, but the reality—and a name that is not merely synonymous but the same name—and to confute it 25 from the propositions granted, necessarily, without including in the reckoning the original point to be proved, in the same respect and relation and manner and time in which it was asserted. A 'false assertion' about anything has to be defined in the same way. Some people, however, omit some one of the said conditions and give a merely apparent refutation, showing (e.g.) that the same thing is both double and not double: for two is double of 30 one, but not double of three. Or, it may be, they show that it is both double and not double of the same thing, but not that it is so in the same respect: for it is double in length but not double in breadth. Or, it may be, they show it to be both double and not double of the same thing and in the same respect and manner, but not that it is so at the same time: and therefore their refutation is merely apparent. One might, with some vio- 35 lence, bring this fallacy into the group of fallacies dependent on language as well.

Those that depend on the assumption of the original point to be proved, occur in the same way, and in as many ways, as it is possible to beg the original point; they appear to refute because men lack the power to keep their eyes at once upon what is the same and what is different.

The refutation which depends upon the consequent arises **167ᵇ**

because people suppose that the relation of consequence is convertible. For whenever, suppose A is, B necessarily is, they
5 then suppose also that if B is, A necessarily is. This is also the source of the deceptions that attend opinions based on sense-perception. For people often suppose bile to be honey because honey is attended by a yellow colour: also, since after rain the ground is wet in consequence, we suppose that if the ground is wet, it has been raining; whereas that does not necessarily follow. In rhetoric proofs from signs are based on consequences.
10 For when rhetoricians wish to show that a man is an adulterer, they take hold of some consequence of an adulterous life, viz. that the man is smartly dressed, or that he is observed to wander about at night. There are, however, many people of whom these things are true, while the charge in question is untrue.

*   *   *

The refutation which depends upon treating as cause what is not a cause, occurs whenever what is not a cause is inserted in the argument, as though the refutation depended upon it. This kind of thing happens in arguments that reason *ad impossibile*: for in these we are bound to demolish one of the premises. If,
25 then, the false cause be reckoned in among the questions that are necessary to establish the resulting impossibility, it will often be thought that the refutation depends upon it. . . . Arguments of that kind, then, though not inconclusive absolutely, are
35 inconclusive in relation to the proposed conclusion. Also even the questioners themselves often fail quite as much to see a point of that kind.

Such, then, are the arguments that depend upon the consequent and upon false cause. Those that depend upon the making of two questions into one occur whenever the plurality is undetected and a single answer is returned as if to a single
168ᵃ question. Now, in some cases, it is easy to see that there is more than one, and that an answer is not to be given, e.g. 'Does the earth consist of sea, or the sky?' But in some cases it is less easy, and then people treat the question as one, and either confess their defeat by failing to answer the question, or are exposed to

an apparent refutation. Thus 'Is *A* and is *B* a man?' 'Yes.' 'Then 5
if any one hits *A* and *B*, he will strike a man' (singular), 'not
men' (plural). Or again, where part is good and part bad, 'is the
whole good or bad?' For whichever he says, it is possible that he
might be thought to expose himself to an apparent refutation or 10
to make an apparently false statement. . . .

The right way, then, is either to divide apparent proofs and
refutations as above, or else to refer them all to ignorance of
what 'refutation' is, and make that our starting-point: for it is
possible to analyse all the aforesaid modes of fallacy into 20
breaches of the definition of a refutation. In the first place, we
may see if they are inconclusive: for the conclusion ought to
result from the premisses laid down, so as to compel us necessarily to state it and not merely to seem to compel us.

*   *   *

Our programme was, then, to discover some faculty of reasoning about any theme put before us from the most generally accepted premisses that there are. For that is the essential task of
the art of discussion (dialectic) and of examination (peirastic).
Inasmuch, however, as it is annexed to it, on account of the 183ᵇ
near presence of the art of sophistry (sophistic), not only to
be able to conduct an examination dialectically but also with a
show of knowledge, we therefore proposed for our treatise not
only the aforesaid aim of being able to exact an account of any
view, but also the aim of ensuring that in standing up to an 5
argument we shall defend our thesis in the same manner by
means of views as generally held as possible. The reason of this
we have explained; for this, too, was why Socrates used to ask
questions and not to answer them; for he used to confess that he
did not know. We have made clear, in the course of what pre-
cedes, the number both of the points with reference to which,
and of the materials from which, this will be accomplished, and
also from what sources we can become well supplied with these: 10
we have shown, moreover, how to question or arrange the ques-
tioning as a whole, and the problems concerning the answers
and solutions to be used against the reasonings of the questioner.

We have also cleared up the problems concerning all other
matters that belong to the same inquiry into arguments. In
15 addition to this we have been through the subject of Fallacies,
as we have already stated above.

That our programme, then, has been adequately completed
is clear. But we must not omit to notice what has happened in
regard to this inquiry. For in the case of all discoveries the results of previous labours that have been handed down from
others have been advanced bit by bit by those who have taken
20 them on, whereas the original discoveries generally make an
advance that is small at first though much more useful than the
development which later springs out of them. For it may be that
in everything, as the saying is, 'the first start is the main part':
and for this reason also it is the most difficult; for in proportion
as it is most potent in its influence, so it is smallest in its com-
25 pass and therefore most difficult to see: whereas when this is once
discovered, it is easier to add and develop the remainder in
connexion with it. This is in fact what has happened in regard
to rhetorical speeches and to practically all the other arts: for
those who discovered the beginnings of them advanced them
30 in all only a little way, whereas the celebrities of to-day are the
heirs (so to speak) of a long succession of men who have advanced them bit by bit, and so have developed them to their
present form, Tisias coming next after the first founders, then
Thrasymachus after Tisias, and Theodorus next to him, while
several people have made their several contributions to it: and
therefore it is not to be wondered at that the art has attained
considerable dimensions. Of this inquiry, on the other hand,
35 it was not the case that part of the work had been thoroughly
done before, while part had not. Nothing existed at all. For the
training given by the paid professors of contentious arguments
was like the treatment of the matter by Gorgias. For they used to
hand out speeches to be learned by heart, some rhetorical, others
in the form of question and answer, each side supposing that
184ᵃ their arguments on either side generally fall among them. And
therefore the teaching they gave their pupils was ready but
rough. For they used to suppose that they trained people by

imparting to them not the art but its products, as though any one professing that he would impart a form of knowledge to obviate any pain in the feet, were then not to teach a man the art 5 of shoe-making or the sources whence he can acquire anything of the kind, but were to present him with several kinds of shoes of all sorts: for he has helped him to meet his need, but has not imparted an art to him. Moreover, on the subject of Rhetoric there exists much that has been said long ago, whereas on the 184 subject of reasoning we had nothing else of an earlier date to speak of at all, but were kept at work for a long time in experimental researches. If, then, it seems to you after inspection that, such being the situation as it existed at the start, our investigation is in a satisfactory condition compared with the other in- 5 quiries that have been developed by tradition, there must remain for all of you, or for our students, the task of extending us your pardon for the shortcomings of the inquiry, and for the discoveries thereof your warm thanks.

JOHN STUART MILL

(1806-1873)

When Mill joined the discussion, the question as to the real basis of the syllogism, whether of a metaphysical, logical, practical, or possibly illusory character had been more or less in dispute for more or less two millenia. On the other hand, the theory of scientific practice had lacked an organizing Newton since the rather haphazard intuitions of Bacon's *Novum Organum*. What Newton did for the practice of scientific theory, Mill did for the theory of scientific practice. (What the twentieth century did to Newton, it did also to Mill.)

A System of Logic: Ratiocinative and Inductive professed, in effect, to be a comprehensive encyclopedia of logical knowledge, laying claim, Mill said, only to such originality as was necessary to effect a coherent synthesis of the achievements of the tradition. The reader detects, however, that there is as much of Mill as of his inheritance in his book, especially in the crucial and best remembered portions, namely, the theory of the syllogism, the canons of induction and the thesis concerning nature's uniformity. If Mill is right, then the traditional syllogism contains inductive inferences in its major premise, its conclusion is tautologous, its real basis lies in metaphysical assumptions, and yet it is scientifically almost indispensable. Important theses, all. But his further, and connected, theory is still bolder: "On the subject of Induction, the task to be performed was that of generalizing the modes of investigating truth and estimating evidence. . . ." What Mill envisaged—in opposition to most of his predecessors and contemporaries—was an ordered, lawful, and exhaustive description of these "modes."

The following sections come from the most perenially interesting chapters in *A System of Logic*. Indeed, a summary of their fundamental ideas has, for a century now, been repeated in almost every English textbook on logic—though frequently as a preliminary to an attempt to show how inadequate Mill's views were. Inadequate they may have been, but they have inspired important new directions of philosophical thought; they have also implanted in most philosophers the conviction that, however induction and deduction are related, they both belong to the business of logic.

RATIOCINATION, OR SYLLOGISM[1]

*　　*　　*

Every proposition which conveys real information asserts a matter of fact, dependent on the laws of nature, and not on classification. It asserts that a given object does or does not possess a given attribute; or it asserts that two attributes, or sets of attributes, do or do not (constantly or occasionally) co-exist. Since such is the purport of all propositions which convey any real knowledge, and since ratiocination is a mode of acquiring real knowledge, any theory of ratiocination which does not recognise this import of propositions, cannot, we may be sure, be the true one.

Applying this view of propositions to the two premises of a syllogism, we obtain the following results. The major premise, which, as already remarked, is always universal, asserts that all things which have a certain attribute (or attributes) have or have not along with it a certain other attribute (or attributes). The minor premise asserts that the thing or set of things which are the subject of that premise have the first-mentioned attribute; and the conclusion is, that they have (or that they have not) the second. Thus in our former example,

All men are mortal,
Socrates is a man,
therefore
Socrates is mortal,

---

[1] The following selections are reprinted from John Stuart Mill, *A System of Logic: Ratiocinative and Inductive* . . . , Eighth edition (London: Longmans, Green & Co., Ltd, 1872). Only some of Mill's footnotes are reproduced.

the subject and predicate of the major premise are connotative terms, denoting objects and connoting attributes. The assertion in the major premise is, that along with one of the two sets of attributes, we always find the other; that the attributes connoted by "man" never exist unless conjoined with the attribute called mortality. The assertion in the minor premise is that the individual named Socrates possesses the former attributes; and it is concluded that he possesses also the attribute mortality. Or if both the premises are general propositions, as—

> All men are mortal,
> All kings are men,
> therefore
> All kings are mortal,

the minor premise asserts that the attributes denoted by kingship only exist in conjunction with those signified by the word "man." The major asserts as before, that the last-mentioned attributes are never found without the attribute of mortality. The conclusion is, that wherever the attributes of kingship are found, that of mortality is found also.

If the major premise were negative, as, No men are omnipotent, it would assert, not that the attributes connoted by "man" never exist without, but that they never exist with, those connoted by "omnipotent:" from which, together with the minor premise, it is concluded that the same incompatibility exists between the attribute omnipotence and those constituting a king. In a similar manner we might analyse any other example of the syllogism.

If we generalise this process, and look out for the principle or law involved in every such inference, and presupposed in every syllogism, the propositions of which are anything more than merely verbal; we find, not the unmeaning *dictum de omni et nullo*,[2] but a fundamental principle, or rather two principles,

---

[2] Mill had said earlier that this thesis had been "erected into a logical maxim, on which all ratiocination is said to be founded, insomuch that to reason and to apply the maxim are supposed to be one and the same thing. The maxim is, That whatever can be affirmed (or denied) of a class, may be affirmed (or denied) of everything included in the class. This axiom, supposed to be the basis of the syllogistic theory, is termed by logicians the *dictum de omni et nullo*." (Editor's note)

strikingly resembling the axioms of mathematics. The first, which is the principle of affirmative syllogism, is, that things which co-exist with the same thing, co-exist with one another: or (still more precisely) a thing which co-exists with another thing, which other co-exists with a third thing, also co-exists with that third thing. The second is the principle of negative syllogisms, and is to this effect: that a thing which co-exists with another thing, with which other a third thing does not co-exist, is not co-existent with that third thing. These axioms manifestly relate to facts, and not to conventions; and one or other of them is the ground of the legitimacy of every argument in which facts and not conventions are the matter treated of.[3]

§4. It remains to translate this exposition of the syllogism from the one into the other of the two languages in which we formerly remarked that all propositions, and of course therefore all combinations of propositions, might be expressed. We observed that a proposition might be considered in two different

---

[3] Mr. Herbert Spencer (*Principles of Psychology*, pp. 125-7) though his theory of the syllogism coincides with all that is essential of mine, thinks it a logical fallacy to present the two axioms in the text as the regulating principles of syllogism. He charges me with falling into the error, pointed out by Archbishop Whately and myself, of confounding exact likeness with literal identity; and maintains that we ought not to say that Socrates possesses *the same* attributes which are connoted by the word Man, but only that he possesses attributes *exactly like* them: according to which phraseology, Socrates and the attribute mortality are not two things co-existing with the same thing, as the axiom asserts, but two things co-existing with two different things.

The question between Mr. Spencer and me is merely one of language; for neither of us (if I understand Mr. Spencer's opinions rightly) believes an attribute to be a real thing, possessed of objective existence; we believe it to be a particular mode of naming our sensations, or our expectations of sensation, when looked at in their relation to an external object which excites them. The question raised by Mr. Spencer does not, therefore, concern the properties of any really existing thing, but the comparative appropriateness, for philosophical purposes, of two different modes of using a name. Considered in this point of view, the phraseology I have employed, which is that commonly used by philosophers, seems to me to be the best. . . .

The meaning of any general name is some outward or inward phenomenon, consisting, in the last resort, of feelings; and these feelings, if their continuity is for an instant broken, are no longer the same feelings, in the sense of individual identity. What, then, is the common something which gives a meaning to the general name? Mr. Spencer can only say, it is the similarity of the feelings: and I rejoin, the attribute is precisely that similarity. The names of attributes are in their ultimate analysis names for the resemblances of **our** sensations (or other feelings). Every general name, whether abstract or **concrete,** denotes or connotes one or more of those resemblances. . . .

lights; as a portion of our knowledge of nature, or as a memorandum for our guidance. Under the former, or speculative aspect, an affirmative general proposition is an assertion of a speculative truth, viz. that whatever has a certain attribute has a certain other attribute. Under the other aspect, it is to be regarded
not as a part of our knowledge, but as an aid for our practical
exigencies, by enabling us, when we see or learn that an object
possesses one of the two attributes, to infer that it possesses the
other; thus employing the first attribute as a mark or evidence of
the second. Thus regarded, every syllogism comes within the
following general formula:—

> Attribute A is a mark of attribute B,
> The given object has the mark A,
> therefore
> The given object has the attribute B.

* * *

To correspond with this alteration in the form of the syllogisms, the axioms on which the syllogistic process is founded
must undergo a corresponding transformation. In this altered
phraseology, both these axioms may be brought under one general expression, namely, that whatever has any mark, has that
which it is a mark of. Or, when the minor premise as well as the
major is universal, we may state it thus: Whatever is a mark of
any mark, is a mark of that which this last is a mark of.

* * *

OF THE FUNCTIONS AND
LOGICAL VALUE OF THE SYLLOGISM

§1. We have shown what is the real nature of the
truths with which the Syllogism is conversant, in contradistinc-

tion to the more superficial manner in which their import is conceived in the common theory; and what are the fundamental axioms on which its probative force or conclusiveness depends. We have now to inquire whether the syllogistic process, that of reasoning from generals to particulars, is, or is not, a process of inference; a process from the known to the unknown: a means of coming to a knowledge of something which we did not know before.

*   *   *

§2. It must be granted that in every syllogism, considered as an argument to prove the conclusion, there is a *petitio principii.* When we say,

All men are mortal,
Socrates is a man,
therefore
Socrates is mortal;

it is unanswerably urged by the adversaries of the syllogistic theory, that the proposition, Socrates is mortal, is presupposed in the more general assumption, All men are mortal: that we cannot be assured of the mortality of all men, unless we are already certain of the mortality of every individual man: that if it be still doubtful whether Socrates, or any other individual we choose to name, be mortal or not, the same degree of uncertainty must hang over the assertion, All men are mortal: that the general principle, instead of being given as evidence of the particular case cannot itself be taken for true without exception, until every shadow of doubt which could affect any case comprised with it, is dispelled by evidence *aliundè;* and then what remains for the syllogism to prove? That, in short, no reasoning from generals to particulars can, as such, prove anything, since from a general principle we cannot infer any particulars, but those which the principle itself assumes as known.

This doctrine appears to me irrefragable; and if logicians, though unable to dispute it, have usually exhibited a strong disposition to explain it away, this was not because they could discover any flaw in the argument itself, but because the ccn-

trary opinion seemed to rest on arguments equally indisputable.
In the syllogism last referred to, for example, or in any of those
which we previously constructed, is it not evident that the conclusion may, to the person to whom the syllogism is presented,
be actually and *bonâ fide* a new truth? Is it not matter of daily
experience that truths previously unthought of, facts which have
not been, and cannot be, directly observed, are arrived at by way
of general reasoning? We believe that the Duke of Wellington
is mortal. We do not know this by direct observation, so long as
he is not yet dead. If we were asked how, this being the case, we
know the Duke to be mortal, we should probably answer, Because all men are so. Here, therefore, we arrive at the knowledge of a truth not (as yet) susceptible of observation, by a reasoning which admits of being exhibited in the following syllogism:—

> All men are mortal,
> The Duke of Wellington is a man,
> therefore
> The Duke of Wellington is mortal.

*   *   *

When you admitted the major premise, you asserted the conclusion; but, says Archbishop Whately, you asserted it by implication merely: this, however, can here only mean that you
asserted it unconsciously; that you did not know you were asserting it; but, if so, the difficulty revives in this shape—Ought you
not to have known? Were you warranted in asserting the general
proposition without having satisfied yourself of the truth of
everything which it fairly includes? And if not, is not the syllogistic art *primâ facie* what its assailants affirm it to be, a contrivance for catching you in a trap, and holding you fast in it?

§3. From this difficulty there appears to be but one issue.
The proposition that the Duke of Wellington is mortal, is evidently an inference; it is got at as a conclusion from something
else; but do we, in reality, conclude it from the proposition, All
men are mortal? I answer, No.

The error committed is, I conceive, that of overlooking the

distinction between two parts of the process of philosophising, the inferring part, and the registering part, and ascribing to the latter the functions of the former. The mistake is that of referring a person to his own notes for the origin of his knowledge. If a person is asked a question, and is at the moment unable to answer it, he may refresh his memory by turning to a memorandum which he carries about with him. But if he were asked, how the fact came to his knowledge, he would scarcely answer, because it was set down in his notebook: unless the book was written, like the Koran, with a quill from the wing of the angel Gabriel.

Assuming that the proposition, The Duke of Wellington is mortal, is immediately an inference from the proposition, All men are mortal; whence do we derive our knowledge of that general truth? Of course from observation. Now, all which man can observe are individual cases. From these all general truths must be drawn, and into these they may be again resolved; for a general truth is but an aggregate of particular truths; a comprehensive expression, by which an indefinite number of individual facts are affirmed or denied at once. But a general proposition is not merely a compendious form for recording and preserving in the memory a number of particular facts, all of which have been observed. Generalisation is not a process of mere naming, it is also a process of inference. From instances which we have observed, we feel warranted in concluding, that what we found true in those instances, holds in all similar ones, past, present, and future, however numerous they may be. We then, by that valuable contrivance of language which enables us to speak of many as if they were one, record all that we have observed, together with all that we infer from our observations, in one concise expression; and have thus only one proposition, instead of an endless number, to remember or to communicate. The results of many observations and inferences, and instructions for making innumerable inferences in unforeseen cases, are compressed into one short sentence.

When, therefore, we conclude from the death of John and Thomas, and every other person we ever heard of in whose case

the experiment had been fairly tried, that the Duke of Wellington is mortal like the rest, we may, indeed, pass through the
generalisation, All men are mortal, as an intermediate stage; but
it is not in the latter half of the process, the descent from all men
to the Duke of Wellington, that the *inference* resides. The inference is finished when we have asserted that all men are mortal. What remains to be performed afterwards is merely de-
ciphering our own notes.

Archbishop Whately has contended that syllogising, or reasoning from generals to particulars, is not, agreeably to the
vulgar idea, a peculiar *mode* of reasoning, but the philosophical
analysis of *the* mode in which all men reason, and must do so if
they reason at all. With the deference due to so high an authority, I cannot help thinking that the vulgar notion is, in this
case, the more correct. If, from our experience of John, Thomas,
&c., who once were living, but are now dead, we are entitled to
conclude that all human beings are mortal, we might surely
without any logical inconsequence have concluded at once from
those instances that the Duke of Wellington is mortal. The mortality of John, Thomas, and others is, after all, the whole evidence we have for the mortality of the Duke of Wellington. Not
one iota is added to the proof by interpolating a general proposition. Since the individual cases are all the evidence we can
possess, evidence which no logical form into which we choose to
throw it can make greater than it is; and since that evidence is
either sufficient in itself, or, if insufficient for the one purpose,
cannot be sufficient for the other; I am unable to see why we
should be forbidden to take the shortest cut from these sufficient premises to the conclusion, and constrained to travel the
"high priori road," by the arbitrary fiat of logicians. I cannot
perceive why it should be impossible to journey from one place
to another unless we "march up a hill, and then march down
again." It may be the safest road, and there may be a resting-
place at the top of the hill, affording a commanding view of the
surrounding country; but for the mere purpose of arriving at
our journey's end, our taking that road is perfectly optional; it
is a question of time, trouble, and danger.

Not only *may* we reason from particulars to particulars without passing through generals, but we perpetually do so reason. All our earliest inferences are of this nature. From the first dawn of intelligence we draw inferences, but years elapse before we learn the use of general language. The child who, having burnt his fingers, avoids to thrust them again into the fire, has reasoned or inferred, though he has never thought of the general maxim, Fire burns. He knows from memory that he has been burnt, and on this evidence believes, when he sees a candle, that if he puts his finger into the flame of it, he will be burnt again. He believes this in every case which happens to arise; but without looking, in each instance, beyond the present case. He is not generalising; he is inferring a particular from particulars. In the same way, also, brutes reason. There is no ground for attributing to any of the lower animals the use of signs of such a nature as to render general propositions possible. But those animals profit by experience, and avoid what they have found to cause them pain, in the same manner, though not always with the same skill, as a human creature. Not only the burnt child, but the burnt dog, dreads the fire.

I believe that, in point of fact, when drawing inferences from our personal experience, and not from maxims handed down to us by books or tradition, we much oftener conclude from particulars to particulars directly, than through the intermediate agency of any general proposition. We are constantly reasoning from ourselves to other people, or from one person to another, without giving ourselves the trouble to erect our observations into general maxims of human or external nature. When we conclude that some person will, on some given occasion, feel or act so and so, we sometimes judge from an enlarged consideration of the manner in which human beings in general, or persons of some particular character, are accustomed to feel and act; but much oftener from merely recollecting the feelings and conduct of the same person in some previous instance, or from considering how we should feel or act ourselves. It is not only the village matron, who, when called to a consultation upon the case of a neighbour's child, pronounces on the evil and its remedy simply on the recollection and authority of what she accounts the similar case of her Lucy. We all, where we have no definite maxims to steer by, guide ourselves in the same way; and if we have an extensive experience, and retain its impressions strongly, we may acquire in this manner a very considerable power of accurate judgment, which we may be utterly incapable of justifying or of communicating to others. Among the higher order of practical intellects there have been many of whom it was remarked how admirably they suited their means to their ends, without being able to give any sufficient reasons for what they did; and applied, or seemed to apply, recondite principles which they were wholly unable to state. This is a natural consequence of having a mind stored with appropriate particulars, and having been long accustomed to reason at once from these to fresh particulars, without practising the habit of stating to oneself or to others the corresponding general propositions.

*   *   *

§4. From the considerations now adduced the following conclusions seem to be established. All inference is from particulars to particulars: General propositions are merely registers of such inferences already made, and short formulæ for making more: The major premise of a syllogism, consequently, is a formula of this description; and the conclusion is not an inference drawn *from* the formula, but an inference drawn *according* to the formula; the real logical antecedent or premise being the particular facts from which the general proposition was collected by induction. Those facts, and the individual instances which supplied them, may have been forgotten; but a record remains, not indeed descriptive of the facts themselves, but showing how those cases may be distinguished, respecting which, the facts, when known, were considered to warrant a given inference. According to the indications of this record we draw our conclusion; which is, to all intents and purposes, a conclusion from the forgotten facts. For this it is essential that we should read the record correctly; and the rules of the syllogism are a set of precautions to ensure our doing so.

This view of the functions of the syllogism is confirmed by the consideration of precisely those cases which might be expected to be least favourable to it, namely, those in which ratiocination is independent of any previous induction. We have already observed that the syllogism, in the ordinary course of our reasoning, is only the latter half of the process of travelling from premises to a conclusion. There are, however, some peculiar cases in which it is the whole process. Particulars alone are capable of being subjected to observation; and all knowledge which is derived from observation begins, therefore, of necessity, in particulars; but our knowledge may, in cases of certain descriptions, be conceived as coming to us from other sources than observation. It may present itself as coming from testimony, which, on the occasion and for the purpose in hand, is accepted as of an authoritative character: and the information thus communicated may be conceived to comprise not only particular facts but general propositions, as when a scientific doctrine is accepted without examination on the authority of writers, or a theological doctrine on that of Scripture. Or the generalisation may not be, in the ordinary sense, an assertion at all, but a command; a law, not in the philosophical, but in the moral and political sense of the term: an expression of the desire of a superior, that we, or any number of other persons, shall conform our conduct to certain general instructions. So far as this asserts a fact, namely, a volition of the legislator, that fact is an individual fact, and the proposition, therefore, is not a general proposition. But the description therein contained of the conduct which it is the will of the legislator that his subject should observe, is general. The proposition asserts, not that all men *are* anything, but that all men *shall* do something.

In both these cases the generalities are the original data, and the particulars are elicited from them by a process which correctly resolves itself into a series of syllogisms. The real nature, however, of the supposed deductive process is evident enough.

The only point to be determined is, whether the authority which declared the general proposition intended to include this case in it; and whether the legislator intended his command to apply to the present case among others or not? This is ascertained by examining whether the case possesses the marks by which, as those authorities have signified, the cases which they meant to certify or to influence may be known. The object of the inquiry is to make out the witness's or the legislator's intention, through the indication given by their words. This is a question, as the Germans express it, of hermeneutics. The operation is not a process of inference, but a process of interpretation.

In this last phrase we have obtained an expression which appears to me to characterise, more aptly than any other, the functions of the syllogism in all cases. When the premises are given by authority, the function of Reasoning is to ascertain the testimony of a witness, or the will of a legislator, by interpreting the signs in which the one has intimated his assertion and the other his command. In like manner, when the premises are derived from observation, the function of Reasoning is to ascertain what we (or our predecessors) formerly thought might be inferred from the observed facts, and to do this by interpreting a memorandum of ours, or of theirs. The memorandum reminds us, that from evidence, more or less carefully weighted, it formerly appeared that a certain attribute might be inferred wherever we perceive a certain mark. The proposition, All men are mortal, for instance, shows that we have had experience from which we thought it followed that the attributes connoted by the term "man" are a mark of mortality. But when we conclude that the Duke of Wellington is mortal, we do not infer this from the memorandum, but from the former experience. All that we infer from the memorandum is our own previous belief (or that of those who transmitted to us the proposition) concerning the inferences which that former experience would warrant.

This view of the nature of the syllogism renders consistent and intelligible what otherwise remains obscure and confused in the theory of Archbishop Whately and other enlightened defenders of the syllogistic doctrine respecting the limits to which its functions are confined. They affirm in as explicit terms as can be used, that the sole office of general reasoning is to prevent inconsistency in our opinions; to prevent us from assenting to anything, the truth of which would contradict something to which we had previously on good grounds given our assent. And they tell us, that the sole ground which a syllogism affords for assenting to the conclusion, is that the supposition of its being false, combined with the supposition that the premises are true, would lead to a contradiction in terms. Now this would be but a lame account of the real grounds which we have for believing the facts which we learn from reasoning, in contradistinction to observation. The true reason why we believe that the Duke of Wellington will die, is that his fathers, and our fathers, and all other persons who were contemporary with them, have died. Those facts are the real premises of the reasoning. But we are not led to infer the conclusion from those premises, by the necessity of avoiding any verbal inconsistency. There is no contradiction in supposing that all those persons have died, and that the Duke of Wellington may, notwithstanding, live for ever. But there would be a contradiction if we first, on the ground of those same premises, made a general assertion including and covering the case of the Duke of Wellington, and then refused to stand to it in the individual case. There is an inconsistency to be avoided between the memorandum we make of the inferences which may be justly drawn in future cases, and the inferences we actually draw in those cases when they arise. With this view we interpret our own formula, precisely as a judge interprets a law; in order that we may avoid drawing any inferences not conformable to our former intention, as a judge avoids giving any decision not conformable to the legislator's intention. The rules for this interpretation are the rules of the syllogism: and its sole purpose is to maintain consistency between the conclusions we draw in every particular case, and the previous general directions for drawing them; whether those general directions were framed by ourselves as the result of induction, or were received by us from an authority competent to give them.

§5. In the above observations it has, I think, been shown, that, though there is always a process of reasoning or inference where a syllogism is used, the syllogism is not a correct analysis of that process of reasoning or inference; which is, on the contrary (when not a mere inference from testimony) an inference from particulars to particulars, authorized by a previous inference from particulars to generals, and substantially the same with it; of the nature, therefore, of Induction. But while these conclusions appear to me undeniable, I must yet enter a protest, as strong as that of Archbishop Whately himself, against the doctrine that the syllogistic art is useless for the purposes of reasoning. The reasoning lies in the act of generalisation, not in interpreting the record of that act; but the syllogistic form is an indispensable collateral security for the correctness of the generalisation itself.

It has already been seen, that if we have a collection of particulars sufficient for grounding an induction, we need not frame a general proposition; we may reason at once from those particulars to other particulars. But it is to be remarked withal, that whenever, from a set of particular cases, we can legitimately draw any inference, we may legitimately make our inference a general one. If, from observation and experiment, we can conclude to one new case, so may we to an indefinite number. If that which has held true in our past experience will therefore hold in time to come, it will not hold merely in some individual case, but in all cases of some given description. Every induction, therefore, which suffices to prove one fact, proves an indefinite multitude of facts: the experience which justifies a single prediction must be such as will suffice to bear out a general theorem. This theorem it is extremely important to ascertain and declare in its broadest form of generality, and thus to place before our minds, in its full extent, the whole of what our evidence must prove if it proves anything.

*   *   *

The value, therefore, of the syllogistic form, and of the rules for using it correctly, does not consist in their being the form and the rules according to which our reasonings are necessarily, or even usually made; but in their furnishing us with a mode in which those reasonings may always be represented, and which is admirably calculated, if they are inconclusive, to bring their inconclusiveness to light. An induction from particulars to generals, followed by a syllogistic process from those generals to other particulars, is a form in which we may always state our reasonings if we please. It is not a form in which we *must* reason, but it is a form in which we may reason, and into which it is indispensable to throw our reasoning when there is any doubt of its validity: though when the case is familiar and little complicated, and there is no suspicion of error, we may, and do, reason at once from the known particular cases to unknown ones.[1]

*   *   *

In the argument, then, which proves that Socrates is mortal, one indispensable part of the premises will be as follows: "My father, and my father's father, A, B, C, and an indefinite number of other persons, were mortal:" which is only an expression in different words of the observed fact that they have died. This is the major premise divested of the *petitio principii,* and cut down to as much as is really known by direct evidence.

In order to connect this proposition with the conclusion Socrates is mortal, the additional link necessary is such a proposition as the following: "Socrates resembles my father, and my father's father, and the other individuals specified." This proposition we assert when we say that Socrates is a man. By saying so we likewise assert in what respect he resembles them, namely,

---

[1] The language of ratiocination would, I think, be brought into closer agreement with the real nature of the process if the general propositions employed in reasoning, instead of being in the form All men are mortal, or Every man is mortal, were expressed in the form Any man is mortal. This mode of expression, exhibiting as the type of all reasoning from experience, "The men A, B, C, &c., are so and so, therefore *any* man is so and so," would much better manifest the true idea—that inductive reasoning is always, at bottom, inference from particulars to particulars, and that the whole function of general propositions in reasoning is to vouch for the legitimacy of such inferences.

in the attributes connoted by the word man. And we conclude
that he further resembles them in the attribute mortality.

§7. We have thus obtained what we were seeking, an universal type of the reasoning process. We find it resolvable in all
cases into the following elements: Certain individuals have a
given attribute; an individual or individuals resemble the
former in certain other attributes; therefore they resemble them
also in the given attribute. This type of ratiocination does not
claim, like the syllogism, to be conclusive from the mere form
of the expression; nor can it possibly be so. That one proposition does or does not assert the very fact which was already asserted in another, may appear from the form of the expression,
that is, from a comparison of the language; but when the two
propositions assert facts which are *bonâ fide* different, whether
the one fact proves the other or not can never appear from the
language, but must depend on other considerations. Whether,
from the attributes in which Socrates resembles those men who
have heretofore died, it is allowable to infer that he resembles
them also in being mortal, is a question of Induction; and is to
be decided by the principles or canons which we shall hereafter
recognize as tests of the correct performance of that great mental
operation.

*   *   *

OF THE GROUND OF INDUCTION

§1. Induction, properly so called, as distinguished
from those mental operations, sometimes though improperly
designated by the name, which I have attempted in the preceding chapter to characterise, may, then, be summarily defined as
Generalisation from Experience. It consists in inferring from

some individual instances in which a phenomenon is observed
to occur, that it occurs in all instances of a certain class; namely,
in all which *resemble* the former, in what are regarded as the
material circumstances.

In what way the material circumstances are to be distinguished from those which are immaterial, or why some of the
circumstances are material and others not so, we are not yet
ready to point out. We must first observe that there is a principle implied in the very statement of what Induction is; an
assumption with regard to the course of nature and the order of
the universe; namely, that there are such things in nature as
parallel cases; that what happens once will, under a sufficient
degree of similarity of circumstances, happen again, and not
only again, but as often as the same circumstances recur. This, I
say, is an assumption involved in every case of induction. And if
we consult the actual course of nature, we find that the assumption is warranted. The universe, so far as known to us, is so constituted, that whatever is true in any one case, is true in all cases
of a certain description; the only difficulty is, to find what description.

This universal fact, which is our warrant for all inferences
from experience, has been described by different philosophers
in different forms of language; that the course of nature is uniform; that the universe is governed by general laws; and the
like.

*   *   *

Whatever be the most proper mode of expressing it, the
proposition that the course of nature is uniform is the fundamental principle, or general axiom, of Induction. It would yet
be a great error to offer this large generalisation as any explanation of the inductive process. On the contrary, I hold it to be
itself an instance of induction, and induction by no means of the
most obvious kind. Far from being the first induction we make,
it is one of the last, or at all events one of those which are latest
in attaining strict philosophical accuracy. As a general maxim,
indeed, it has scarcely entered into the minds of any but phi-

losophers; nor even by them, as we shall have many opportunities of remarking, have its extent and limits been always very justly conceived. The truth is, that this great generalisation is itself founded on prior generalisations. The obscurer laws of nature were discovered by means of it, but the more obvious ones must have been understood and assented to as general truths before it was ever heard of. We should never have thought of affirming that all phenomena take place according to general laws, if we had not first arrived, in the case of a great multitude of phenomena, at some knowledge of the laws themselves; which could be done no otherwise than by induction. In what sense, then, can a principle, which is so far from being our earliest induction, be regarded as our warrant for all the others? In the only sense in which (as we have already seen) the general propositions which we place at the head of our reasonings when we throw them into syllogisms ever really contribute to their validity. As Archbishop Whately remarks, every induction is a syllogism with the major premise suppressed; or (as I prefer expressing it) every induction may be thrown into the form of a syllogism by supplying a major premise. If this be actually done, the principle which we are now considering, that of the uniformity of the course of nature, will appear as the ultimate major premise of all inductions, and will, therefore, stand to all inductions in the relation in which, as has been shown at so much length, the major proposition of a syllogism always stands to the conclusion; not contributing at all to prove it, but being a necessary condition of its being proved; since no conclusion is proved for which there cannot be found a true major premise.

The statement that the uniformity of the course of nature is the ultimate major premise in all cases of induction may be thought to require some explanation. The immediate major premise in every inductive argument it certainly is not. Of that Archbishop Whately's must be held to be the correct account. The induction, "John, Peter, &c., are mortal, therefore all mankind are mortal," may, as he justly says, be thrown into a syllogism by prefixing as a major premise, (what is at any rate a necessary condition of the validity of the argument,) namely, that what is true of John, Peter, &c., is true of all mankind. But how came we by this major premise? It is not self-evident; nay, in all cases of unwarranted generalisation it is not true. How, then, is it arived at? Necessarily either by induction or ratiocination; and if by induction, the process, like all other inductive arguments, may be thrown into the form of a syllogism. This previous syllogism it is, therefore, necessary to construct. There is, in the long-run, only one possible construction. The real proof that what is true of John, Peter, &c., is true of all mankind, can only be, that a different supposition would be inconsistent with the uniformity which we know to exist in the course of nature. Whether there would be this inconsistency or not, may be a matter of long and delicate inquiry; but unless there would, we have no sufficient ground for the major of the inductive syllogism. It hence appears, that if we throw the whole course of any inductive argument into a series of syllogisms, we shall arrive by more or fewer steps at an ultimate syllogism, which will have for its major premise the principle or axiom of the uniformity of the course of nature.[1]

*　　*　　*

---

[1] But though it is a condition of the validity of every induction that there be uniformity in the course of nature, it is not a necessary condition that the uniformity should pervade all nature. It is enough that it pervades the particular class of phenomena to which the induction relates. An induction concerning the motions of the planets, or the properties of the magnet, would not be vitiated though we were to suppose that wind and weather are the sport of chance, provided it be assumed that astronomical and magnetic phenomena are under the dominion of general laws. Otherwise the early experience of mankind would have rested on a very weak foundation; for in the infancy of science it could not be known that *all* phenomena are regular in their course.

Neither would it be correct to say that every induction by which we infer any truth implies the general fact of uniformity *as foreknown,* even in reference to the kind of phenomena concerned. It implies, *either* that this general fact is already known, *or* that we may now know it. . . .

OF THE FOUR METHODS
OF EXPERIMENTAL INQUIRY

§1. The simplest and most obvious modes of singling
out from among the circumstances which precede or follow a
phenomenon those with which it is really connected by an invariable law are two in number. One is, by comparing together
different instances in which the phenomenon occurs. The other
is, by comparing instances in which the phenomenon does occur, with instances in other respects similar in which it does
not. These two methods may be respectively denominated the
Method of Agreement and the Method of Difference.

*   *   *

We shall denote antecedents by the large letters of the alpha-
bet, and the consequents corresponding to them by the small.
Let A, then, be an agent or cause, and let the object of our inquiry be to ascertain what are the effects of this cause. If we can
either find or produce the agent A in such varieties of circumstances that the different cases have no circumstance in common
except A, then whatever effect we find to be produced in all our
trials is indicated as the effect of A. Suppose, for example, that
A is tried along with B and C, and that the effect is *a b c*; and
suppose that A is next tried with D and E, but without B and
C, and that the effect is *a d e*. Then we may reason thus: *b* and
c are not effects of A, for they were not produced by it in the
second experiment; nor are *d* and *e*, for they were not produced
in the first. Whatever is really the effect of A must have been
produced in both instances; now this condition is fulfilled by
no circumstance except *a*. The phenomenon *a* cannot have been

the effect of B or C, since it was produced where they were not; nor of D or E, since it was produced where they were not. Therefore it is the effect of A.

For example, let the antecedent A be the contact of an alkaline substance and an oil. This combination being tried under several varieties of circumstances, resembling each other in nothing else, the results agree in the production of a greasy and detersive or saponaceous substance: it is therefore concluded that the combination of an oil and an alkali causes the production of a soap. It is thus we inquire, by the Method of Agreement, into the effect of a given cause.

In a similar manner we may inquire into the cause of a given effect. Let *a* be the effect. Here, as shown in the last chapter, we have only the resource of observation without experiment: we cannot take a phenomenon of which we know not the origin, and try to find its mode of production by producing it: if we succeeded in such a random trial it could only be by accident. But if we can observe *a* in two different combinations, *a b c* and *a d e*; and if we know, or can discover, that the antecedent circumstances in these cases respectively were A B C and A D E, we may conclude by a reasoning similar to that in the preceding example, that A is the antecedent connected with the consequent *a* by a law of causation. B and C, we may say, cannot be causes of *a*, since on its second occurrence they were not present; nor are D and E, for they were not present on its first occurrence. A, alone of the five circumstances, was found among the antecedents of *a* in both instances.

*   *   *

The mode of discovering and proving laws of nature, which we have now examined, proceeds on the following axiom. Whatever circumstances can be excluded, without prejudice to the phenomenon, or can be absent notwithstanding its presence, is not connected with it in the way of causation. The casual circumstance being thus eliminated, if only one remains, that one is the cause which we are in search of: if more than one, they either are, or contain among them, the cause; and so, *mutatis mutandis,* of the effect. As this method proceeds by comparing different instances to ascertain in what they agree, I have termed it the Method of Agreement; and we may adopt as its regulating principle the following canon:—

FIRST CANON

If two or more instances of the phenomenon under investigation have only one circumstance in common, the circumstance in which alone all the instances agree is the cause (or effect) of the given phenomenon.

Quitting for the present the Method of Agreement, to which we shall almost immediately return, we proceed to a still more potent instrument of the investigation of nature, the Method of Difference.

§2. In the Method of Agreement, we endeavoured to obtain instances which agreed in the given circumstance but differed in every other: in the present method we require, on the contrary, two instances resembling one another in every other respect, but differing in the presence or absence of the phenomenon we wish to study. If our object be to discover the effects of an agent A, we must procure A in some set of ascertained circumstances, as A B C, and having noted the effects produced, compare them with the effect of the remaining circumstances B C, when A is absent. If the effect of A B C is *a b c,* and the effect of B C, *b c,* it is evident that the effect of A is *a.* So again, if we begin at the other end, and desire to investigate the cause of an effect *a,* we must select an instance, as *a b c,* in which the effect occurs, and in which the antecedents were A B C, and we must look out for another instance in which the remaining circumstances, *b c,* occur without *a.* If the antecedents, in that instance, are B C, we know that the cause of *a* must be A: either A alone, or A in conjunction with some of the other circumstances present.

It is scarcely necessary to give examples of a logical process to which we owe almost all the inductive conclusions we draw in early life. When a man is shot through the heart, it is by this method we know that it was the gunshot which killed him: for he was in the fulness of life immediately before, all circumstances being the same, except the wound.

The axioms implied in this method are evidently the following. Whatever antecedent cannot be excluded without preventing the phenomenon, is the cause, or a condition of that phenomenon: Whatever consequent can be excluded, with no other difference in the antecedents than the absence of a particular one, is the effect of that one. Instead of comparing different instances of a phenomenon, to discover in what they agree, this method compares an instance of its occurrence with an instance of its non-occurrence, to discover in what they differ. The canon which is the regulating principle of the Method of Difference may be expressed as follows:—

SECOND CANON

If an instance in which the phenomenon under investigation occurs, and an instance in which it does not occur, have every circumstance in common save one, that one occurring only in the former; the circumstance in which alone the two instances differ is the effect, or the cause, or an indispensable part of the cause, of the phenomenon.

§3. The two methods which we have now stated have many features of resemblance, but there are also many distinctions between them. Both are methods of *elimination*. This term (employed in the theory of equations to denote the process by which one after another of the elements of a question is excluded, and the solution made to depend on the relation between the remaining elements only) is well suited to express the operation, analogous to this, which has been understood since the time of Bacon to be the foundation of experimental inquiry, namely, the successive exclusion of the various circumstances which are found to accompany a phenomenon in a given instance, in order to ascertain what are those among them which can be absent consistently with the existence of the phenomenon. The Method of Agreement stands on the ground that whatever can be eliminated is not connected with the phenomenon by any law. The Method of Difference has for its foundation, that whatever cannot be eliminated is connected with the phenomenon by a law.

*   *   *

It thus appears to be by the Method of Difference alone that we can ever, in the way of direct experience, arrive with certainty at causes. The Method of Agreement leads only to laws of phenomena, (as some writers call them, but improperly, since laws of causation are also laws of phenomena,) that is, to uniformities, which either are not laws of causation, or in which the question of causation must for the present remain undecided. The Method of Agreement is chiefly to be resorted to as a means of suggesting applications of the Method of Difference, (as in the last example the comparison of A B C, A D E, A F G, suggested that A was the antecedent on which to try the experiment whether it could produce *a*,) or as an inferior resource in case the Method of Difference is impracticable; which, as we before showed, generally arises from the impossibility of artificially producing the phenomena. And hence it is that the Method of Agreement, though applicable in principle to either case, is more emphatically the method of investigation on those subjects where artificial experimentation is impossible; because on those it is generally our only resource of a directly inductive nature; while, in the phenomena which we can produce at pleasure, the Method of Difference generally affords a more efficacious process, which will ascertain causes as well as mere laws.

§4. There are, however, many cases in which, though our power of producing the phenomenon is complete, the Method of Difference either cannot be made available at all, or not without a previous employment of the Method of Agreement. This occurs when the agency by which we can produce the phenomenon is not that of one single antecedent, but a combination of antecedents, which we have no power of separating from each other and exhibiting apart. For instance, suppose the subject of inquiry to be the cause of the double refraction of light. We can produce this phenomenon at pleasure by employing any one of the many substances which are known to refract light in that peculiar manner. But if, taking one of those substances, as Iceland spar, for example, we wish to determine on which of the properties of Iceland spar this remarkable phenomenon depends, we can make no use for that purpose of the Method of Difference; for we cannot find another substance precisely resembling Iceland spar except in some one property. The only mode, therefore, of prosecuting this inquiry is that afforded by the Method of Agreement; by which, in fact, through a comparison of all the known substances which have the property of doubly refracting light, it was ascertained that they agree in the circumstance of being crystalline substances; and though the converse does not hold, though all crystalline substances have not the property of double refraction, it was concluded, with reason, that there is a real connection between these two properties; that either crystalline structure, or the cause which gives rise to that structure, is one of the conditions of double refraction.

Out of this employment of the Method of Agreement arises a peculiar modification of that method, which is sometimes of great avail in the investigation of nature. In cases similar to the above, in which it is not possible to obtain the precise pair of instances which our second canon requires—instances agreeing in every antecedent except A, or in every consequent except *a* —we may yet be able, by a double employment of the Method of Agreement, to discover in what the instances which contain A or *a* differ from those which do not.

If we compare various instances in which *a* occurs, and find that they all have in common the circumstance A, and (as far as can be observed) no other circumstance, the Method of Agreement, so far, bears testimony to a connection between A and *a*. In order to convert this evidence of connection into proof of causation by the direct Method of Difference, we ought to be able, in some one of these instances, as, for example, A B C, to leave out A, and observe whether by doing so *a* is prevented. Now supposing (what is often the case) that we are not able to try this decisive experiment, yet, provided we can by any means discover what would be its result if we could try it, the advantage will be the same. Suppose, then, that as we previously examined a variety of instances in which *a* occurred, and found them to agree in containing A, so we now observe a variety of instances in which *a* does not occur, and find them agree in not containing A; which establishes, by the Method of Agreement, the same connection between the absence of A and the absence of *a*, which was before established between their presence. As, then, it had been shown that whenever A is present *a* is present, so it being now shown that when A is taken away *a* is removed along with it, we have by the one proposition A B C, *a b c*, by the other B C, *b c*, the positive and negative instances which the Method of Difference requires.

This method may be called the Indirect Method of Difference, or the Joint Method of Agreement and Difference, and consists in a double employment of the Method of Agreement, each proof being independent of the other, and corroborating it. But it is not equivalent to a proof by the direct Method of Difference. For the requisitions of the Method of Difference are not satisfied unless we can be quite sure either that the instances affirmative of *a* agree in no antecedent whatever but A, or that the instances negative of *a* agree in nothing but the negation of A. Now if it were possible, which it never is, to have this assurance, we should not need the joint method; for either of the two sets of instances separately would then be sufficient to prove causation. This indirect method, therefore, can only be regarded as a great extension and improvement of the Method of Agreement, but not as participating in the more cogent nature of the Method of Difference. The following may be stated as its canon:—

THIRD CANON

If two or more instances in which the phenomenon occurs have only one circumstance in common, while two or more instances in which it does not occur have nothing in common save the absence of that circumstance, the circumstance in which alone the two sets of instances differ is the effect, or the cause, or an indispensable part of the cause, of the phenomenon.

We shall presently see that the Joint Method of Agreement and Difference constitutes, in another respect not yet adverted to, an improvement upon the common Method of Agreement, namely, in being unaffected by a characteristic imperfection of that method, the nature of which still remains to be pointed out. But as we cannot enter into this exposition without introducing a new element of complexity into this long and intricate discussion, I shall postpone it to a subsequent chapter, and shall at once proceed to a statement of two other methods, which will complete the enumeration of the means which mankind possess for exploring the laws of nature by specific observation and experience.

§5. The first of these has been aptly denominated the Method of Residues. Its principle is very simple. Subducting from any given phenomenon all the portions which, by virtue of preceding inductions, can be assigned to known causes, the remainder will be the effect of the antecedents which had been overlooked, or of which the effect was as yet an unknown quantity.

Suppose, as before, that we have the antecedents A B C, followed by the consequents *a b c,* and that by previous inductions (founded, we will suppose, on the Method of Difference) we have ascertained the causes of some of these effects, or the effects of some of these causes; and are thence apprised that the effect of A is *a,* and that the effect of B is *b.* Subtracting the sum of these effects from the total phenomenon, there remains *c,* which now, without any fresh experiments, we may know to be the effect of C. This Method of Residues is in truth a peculiar modification of the Method of Difference. If the instance A B C, *a b c,* could have been compared with a single instance A B, *a b,* we should have proved C to be the cause of *c,* by the common process of the Method of Difference. In the present case, however, instead of a single instance A B, we have had to study separately the causes A and B, and to infer from the effects which they produce separately what effect they must produce in the case A B C where they act together. Of the two instances, therefore, which the Method of Difference requires,—the one positive, the other negative,—the negative one, or that in which the given phenomenon is absent, is not the direct result of observation and experiment, but has been arrived at by deduction. As one of the forms of the Method of Difference, the Method of Residues partakes of its rigorous certainty, provided the previous inductions, those which gave the effects of A and B, were obtained by the same infallible method, and provided we are certain that C is the *only* antecedent to which the residual phenomenon *c* can be referred; the only agent of which we had not already calculated and subducted the effect. But as we can never be quite certain of this, the evidence derived from the Method of Residues is not complete unless we can obtain C artificially and try it separately, or unless its agency, when once suggested, can be accounted for, and proved deductively, from known laws.

Even with these reservations, the Method of Residues is one of the most important among our instruments of discovery. Of all the methods of investigating laws of nature, this is the most fertile in unexpected results: often informing us of sequences in which neither the cause nor the effect were sufficiently conspicuous to attract of themselves the attention of observers. The agent C may be an obscure circumstance, not likely to have been perceived unless sought for, nor likely to have been sought for until attention had been awakened by the insufficiency of the obvious causes to account for the whole of the effect. And *c* may be so disguised by its intermixture with *a* and *b*, that it would scarcely have presented itself spontaneously as a subject of separate study. Of these uses of the method we shall presently cite some remarkable examples. The canon of the Method of Residues is as follows:—

FOURTH CANON

Subduct from any phenomenon such part as is known by previous inductions to be the effect of certain antecedents, and the residue of the phenomenon is the effect of the remaining antecedents.

§6. There remains a class of laws which it is impracticable to ascertain by any of the three methods which I have attempted to characterise, namely, the laws of those Permanent Causes, or indestructible natural agents, which it is impossible either to exclude or to isolate; which we can neither hinder from being present, nor contrive that they shall be present alone. It would appear at first sight that we could by no means separate the effects of these agents from the effects of those other phenomena with which they cannot be prevented from co-existing.

*   *   *

As another example, let us take the phenomenon Heat. Independently of all hypothesis as to the real nature of the agency so called, this fact is certain, that we are unable to exhaust any body of the whole of its heat. It is equally certain that no one ever perceived heat not emanating from a body. Being unable, then, to separate Body and Heat, we cannot effect such a variation of circumstances as the foregoing three methods require; we cannot ascertain, by those methods, what portion of the phenomena exhibited by any body is due to the heat contained in it. If we could observe a body with its heat, and the same body entirely divested of heat, the Method of Difference would show the effect due to the heat, apart from that due to the body. If we could observe heat under circumstances agreeing in nothing but heat, and therefore not characterised also by the presence of a body, we could ascertain the effects of heat, from an instance of heat with a body and an instance of heat without a body, by the Method of Agreement; or we could determine by the Method of Difference what effect was due to the body, when the remainder which was due to the heat would be given by the Method of Residues. But we can do none of these things; and without them the application of any of the three methods to the solution of this problem would be illusory. It would be idle, for instance, to attempt to ascertain the effect of heat by subtracting from the phenomena exhibited by a body all that is due to its other properties; for as we have never been able to observe any bodies without a portion of heat in them, effects due to that heat might form a part of the very results which we were affecting to subtract in order that the effect of heat might be shown by the residue.

If, therefore, there were no other methods of experimental investigation than these three, we should be unable to determine the effects due to heat as a cause. But we have still a resource. Though we cannot exclude an antecedent altogether, we may be able to produce, or nature may produce for us, some modification in it. By a modification is here meant a change in it, not amounting to its total removal. If some modification in the antecedent A is always followed by a change in the consequent *a*, the other consequents *b* and *c* remaining the same; or *vice versâ*, if every change in *a* is found to have been preceded by some modification in A, none being observable in any of the other antecedents; we may safely conclude that *a* is, wholly or in part, an effect traceable to A, or at least in some way connected with it through causation. For example, in the case of heat, though we cannot expel it altogether from any body, we can modify it in quantity, we can increase or diminish it; and doing so, we find by the various methods of experimentation or observation already treated of, that such increase or diminution of heat is followed by expansion or contraction of the body. In this manner we arrive at the conclusion, otherwise unattainable by us, that one of the effects of heat is to enlarge the dimensions of bodies; or what is the same thing in other words, to widen the distances between their particles.

*   *   *

That the oscillations of the pendulum are caused by the earth is proved by similar evidence. Those oscillations take place between equidistant points on the two sides of a line, which, being perpendicular to the earth, varies with every variation in the earth's position, either in space or relatively to the object. Speaking accurately, we only know by the method now characterised that all terrestrial bodies tend to the earth, and not to some unknown fixed point lying in the same direction. In every twenty-four hours, by the earth's rotation, the line drawn from the body at right angles to the earth coincides successively with all the radii of a circle, and in the course of six months the place of that circle varies by nearly two hundred millions of miles; yet

in all these changes of the earth's position, the line in which
bodies tend to fall continues to be directed towards it: which
proves that terrestrial gravity is directed to the earth, and not,
as was once fancied by some, to a fixed point of space.

The method by which these results were obtained may be
termed the Method of Concomitant Variations: it is regulated
by the following canon:—

FIFTH CANON

Whatever phenomenon varies in any manner whenever an-
other phenomenon varies in some particular manner, is either
a cause or an effect of that phenomenon, or is connected with
it through some fact of causation.

The last clause is subjoined because it by no means follows,
when two phenomena accompany each other in their variations,
that the one is cause and the other effect. The same thing may,
and indeed must happen, supposing them to be two different
effects of a common cause: and by this method alone it would
never be possible to ascertain which of the suppositions is the
true one. The only way to solve the doubt would be that which
we have so often adverted to, viz. by endeavouring to ascertain
whether we can produce the one set of variations by means of
the other. In the case of heat, for example, by increasing the
temperature of a body we increase its bulk, but by increasing
its bulk we do not increase its temperature; on the contrary, (as
in the rarefaction of air under the receiver of an air-pump,) we
generally diminish it: therefore heat is not an effect, but a cause,
of increase of bulk. If we cannot ourselves produce the variations, we must endeavour, though it is an attempt which is sel-
dom successful, to find them produced by nature in some case
in which the pre-existing circumstances are perfectly known to
us.

It is scarcely necessary to say, that in order to ascertain the
uniform concomitants of variations in the effect with variations
in the cause, the same precautions must be used as in any other
case of the determination of an invariable sequence. We must
endeavour to retain all the other antecedents unchanged, while

that particular one is subjected to the requisite series of variations; or, in other words, that we may be warranted in inferring
causation from concomitance of variations, the concomitance
itself must be proved by the Method of Difference.

*   *   *

Although the most striking applications of the Method of
Concomitant Variations take place in the cases in which the
Method of Difference, strictly so called, is impossible, its use is
not confined to those cases; it may often usefully follow after
the Method of Difference, to give additional precision to a solution which that has found. When by the Method of Difference it has first been ascertained that a certain object produces
a certain effect, the Method of Concomitant Variations may be
usefully called in to determine according to what law the quantity or the different relations of the effect follow those of the
cause.

§7. The case in which this method admits of the most extensive employment is that in which the variations of the cause are
variations of quantity. Of such variations we may in general
affirm with safety that they will be attended not only with variations, but with similar variations of the effect: the proposition,
that more of the cause is followed by more of the effect, being
a corollary from the principle of the Composition of Causes,
which, as we have seen, is the general rule of causation; cases
of the opposite description, in which causes change their properties on being conjoined with one another, being, on the contrary, special and exceptional. Suppose, then, that when A
changes in quantity, *a* also changes in quantity, and in such a
manner that we can trace the numerical relation which the
changes of the one bear to such changes of the other as take
place within our limits of observation. We may then, with certain precautions, safely conclude that the same numerical relation will hold beyond those limits. If, for instance, we find that
when A is double, *a* is double; that when A is treble or quadruple, *a* is treble or quadruple; we may conclude that if A were

a half or a third, *a* would be a half or a third; and finally, that if A were annihilated, *a* would be annihilated; and that *a* is wholly the effect of A, or wholly the effect of the same cause with A. And so with any other numerical relation according to which A and *a* would vanish simultaneously; as, for instance, if *a* were proportional to the square of A. If, on the other hand, *a* is not wholly the effect of A, but yet varies when A varies, it is probably a mathematical function not of A alone, but of A and something else; its changes, for example, may be such as would occur if part of it remained constant, or varied on some other principle, and the remainder varied in some numerical relation to the variations of A. In that case, when A diminishes, *a* will be seen to approach not towards zero, but towards some other limit; and when the series of variations is such as to indicate what that limit is, if constant, or the law of its variation if variable, the limit will exactly measure how much of *a* is the effect of some other and independent cause, and the remainder will be the effect of A (or of the cause of A).

These conclusions, however, must not be drawn without certain precautions. In the first place, the possibility of drawing them at all manifestly supposes that we are acquainted not only with the variations, but with the absolute quantities both of A and *a*. If we do not know the total quantities, we cannot, of course, determine the real numerical relation according to which those quantities vary. It is therefore an error to conclude, as some have concluded, that because increase of heat expands bodies, that is, increases the distance between their particles, therefore the distance is wholly the effect of heat, and that if we could entirely exhaust the body of its heat, the particles would be in complete contact. This is no more than a guess, and of the most hazardous sort, not a legitimate induction; for since we neither know how much heat there is in any body, nor what is the real distance between any two of its particles, we cannot judge whether the contraction of the distance does or does not follow the diminution of the quantity of heat according to such a numerical relation that the two quantities would vanish simultaneously.

*   *   *

There is also another characteristic uncertainty affecting the inference that the law of variation, which the quantities observe within our limits of observation, will hold beyond those limits. There is, of course, in the first instance, the possibility that beyond the limits, and in circumstances therefore of which we have no direct experience, some counteracting cause might develop itself; either a new agent, or a new property of the agents concerned, which lies dormant in the circumstances we are able to observe. This is an element of uncertainty which enters largely into all our predictions of effects; but it is not peculiarly applicable to the Method of Concomitant Variations. The uncertainty, however, of which I am about to speak is characteristic of that method, especially in the cases in which the extreme limits of our observation are very narrow in comparison with the possible variations in the quantities of the phenomena. Any one who has the slightest acquaintance with mathematics is aware that very different laws of variation may produce numerical results which differ but slightly from one another within narrow limits; and it is often only when the absolute amounts of variation are considerable that the difference between the results given by one law and by another becomes appreciable. When, therefore, such variations in the quantity of the antecedents as we have the means of observing are small in comparison with the total quantities, there is much danger lest we should mistake the numerical law, and be led to miscalculate the variations which would take place beyond the limits; a miscalculation which would vitiate any conclusion respecting the dependence of the effect upon the cause, that could be founded on those variations. Examples are not wanting of such mistakes. . . .

In this uncertainty, the conclusion we may draw from the concomitant variations of a and A, to the existence of an invariable and exclusive connection between them, or to the permanency of the same numerical relation between their variations when the quantities are much greater or smaller than those which we have had the means of observing, cannot be considered to rest on a complete induction. All that in such a case can be regarded as proved on the subject of causation is, that there is some connection between the two phenomena; that A, or something which can influence A, must be *one* of the causes which collectively determine *a*. We may, however, feel assured that the relation which we have observed to exist between the variations of A and *a*, will hold true in all cases which fall between the same extreme limits; that is, wherever the utmost increase or diminution in which the result has been found by observation to coincide with the law, is not exceeded.

The four methods which it has now been attempted to describe are the only possible modes of experimental inquiry—of direct induction *à posteriori*, as distinguished from deduction: at least, I know not, nor am able to imagine, any others. And even of these, the Method of Residues, as we have seen, is not independent of deduction; though, as it also requires specific experience, it may, without impropriety, be included among methods of direct observation and experiment.

These, then, with such assistance as can be obtained from Deduction, compose the available resources of the human mind for ascertaining the laws of the succession of phenomena.

*   *   *

LEWIS CARROLL

(1832-1898)

Lewis Carroll's contributions to logic were rather indirect: as professor of mathematics (C. L. Dodgson), as the source of countless often repeated textbook examples, and as the author of that ageless entertainer, *Alice's Adventures in Wonderland*. He skirted logic with several books on mathematics and several more on lighter subjects. One of his powers lay in his sure eye for the slightly eccentric application of logic both to ordinary life and to the theories of the philosophers, frequently the sort of application that contained an explosive challenge to some little reigning dogma. The following selection is not merely a comic interlude.

WHAT THE TORTOISE SAID TO ACHILLES[1]

Achilles had overtaken the Tortoise, and had seated himself comfortably on its back.

"So you've got to the end of our race-course?" said the Tortoise. "Even though it *does* consist of an infinite series of distances? I thought some wiseacre or other had proved that the thing couldn't be done?"

"It *can* be done," said Achilles. "It *has* been done! *Solvitur ambulando.* You see the distances were constantly *diminishing;* and so—"

[1] Reprinted from Lewis Carroll, *Mind*, N.S. IV, No. 14 (April 1895), 278-280.

"But if they had been constantly *increasing?*" the Tortoise interrupted. "How then?"

"Then I shouldn't be *here*," Achilles modestly replied; "and *you* would have got several times round the world, by this time!"

"You flatter me—*flatten*, I mean," said the Tortoise; "for you *are* a heavy weight, and *no* mistake! Well now, would you like to hear of a race-course, that most people fancy they can get to the end of in two or three steps, while it *really* consists of an infinite number of distances, each one longer than the previous one?"

"Very much indeed!" said the Grecian warrior, as he drew from his helmet (few Grecian warriors possessed *pockets* in those days) an enormous note-book and a pencil. "Proceed! And speak *slowly*, please! *Shorthand* isn't invented yet!"

"That beautiful First Proposition of Euclid!" the Tortoise murmured dreamily. "You admire Euclid?"

"Passionately! So far, at least, as one *can* admire a treatise that won't be published for some centuries to come!"

"Well, now, let's take a little bit of the argument in that First Proposition—just *two* steps, and the conclusion drawn from them. Kindly enter them in your note-book. And in order to refer to them conveniently, let's call them *A, B,* and *Z*:—

(*A*) Things that are equal to the same are equal to each other.

(*B*) The two sides of this Triangle are things that are equal to the same.

(*Z*) The two sides of this Triangle are equal to each other.

Readers of Euclid will grant, I suppose, that *Z* follows logically from *A* and *B*, so that any one who accepts *A* and *B* as true, *must* accept *Z* as true?"

"Undoubtedly! The youngest child in a High School—as soon as High Schools are invented, which will not be till some two thousand years later—will grant *that*."

"And if some reader had *not* yet accepted *A* and *B* as true, he might still accept the *sequence* as a *valid* one, I suppose?"

"No doubt such a reader might exist. He might say 'I accept as true the Hypothetical Proposition that, *if A* and *B* be true, *Z* must be true; but, I *don't* accept *A* and *B* as true.' Such a reader would do wisely in abandoning Euclid, and taking to football."

"And might there not *also* be some reader who would say 'I accept *A* and *B* as true, but I *don't* accept the Hypothetical'?"

"Certainly there might. *He,* also, had better take to football."

"And *neither* of these readers," the Tortoise continued, "is *as yet* under any logical necessity to accept *Z* as true?"

"Quite so," Achilles assented.

"Well, now, I want you to consider *me* as a reader of the *second* kind, and to force me, logically, to accept *Z* as true."

"A tortoise playing football would be—" Achilles was beginning   ,Deviation from the normal rule

"—an anomaly, of course," the Tortoise hastily interrupted. "Don't wander from the point. Let's have *Z* first, and football afterwards!"

"I'm to force you to accept *Z*, am I?" Achilles said musingly. "And your present position is that you accept *A* and *B*, but you *don't* accept the Hypothetical—"

"Let's call it *C*," said the Tortoise.

"—but you *don't* accept

(*C*) If *A* and *B* are true, *Z* must be true."

"That is my present position," said the Tortoise.

"Then I must ask you to accept *C*."

"I'll do so," said the Tortoise, "as soon as you've entered it in that note-book of yours. What else have you got in it?"

"Only a few memoranda," said Achilles, nervously fluttering the leaves: "a few memoranda of—of the battles in which I have distinguished myself!"

"Plenty of blank leaves, I see!" the Tortoise cheerily remarked. "We shall need them *all!*" (Achilles shuddered.) "Now write as I dictate:—

(*A*) Things that are equal to the same are equal to each other.

(*B*) The two sides of this Triangle are things that are equal to the same.

(*C*) If *A* and *B* are true, *Z* must be true.

(*Z*) The two sides of this Triangle are equal to each other."

"You should call it *D*, not *Z*," said Achilles. "It comes *next* to the other three. If you accept *A* and *B* and *C*, you *must* accept *Z*."

"And why *must* I?"

"Because it follows *logically* from them. If *A* and *B* and *C* are true, *Z* *must* be true. You don't dispute *that*, I imagine?"

"If *A* and *B* and *C* are true, *Z* *must* be true," the Tortoise thoughtfully repeated. "That's *another* Hypothetical, isn't it? And, if I failed to see its truth, I might accept *A* and *B* and *C*, and *still* not accept *Z*, mightn't I?"

"You might," the candid hero admitted; "though such obtuseness would certainly be phenomenal. Still, the event is *possible*. So I must ask you to grant *one* more Hypothetical."

"Very good. I'm quite willing to grant it, as soon as you've written it down. We will call it

(*D*) If *A* and *B* and *C* are true, *Z* must be true.

Have you entered that in your note-book?"

"I *have!*" Achilles joyfully exclaimed, as he ran the pencil into its sheath. "And at last we've got to the end of this ideal race-course! Now that you accept *A* and *B* and *C* and *D*, *of course* you accept *Z*."

"Do I?" said the Tortoise innocently. "Let's make that quite clear. I accept *A* and *B* and *C* and *D*. Suppose I *still* refused to accept *Z*?"

"Then Logic would take you by the throat, and *force* you to do it!" Achilles triumphantly replied. "Logic would tell you 'You can't help yourself. Now that you've accepted *A* and *B* and *C* and *D*, you *must* accept *Z*!' So you've no choice, you see."

"Whatever *Logic* is good enough to tell me is worth *writing down*," said the Tortoise. "So enter it in your book, please. We will call it

(*E*) If *A* and *B* and *C* and *D* are true, *Z* must be true. Until I've granted *that*, of course I needn't grant *Z*. So it's quite a *necessary* step, you see?"

"I see," said Achilles; and there was a touch of sadness in his tone.

Here the narrator, having pressing business at the Bank, was obliged to leave the happy pair, and did not again pass the spot until some months afterwards. When he did so, Achilles was still seated on the back of the much-enduring Tortoise, and was writing in his note-book, which appeared to be nearly full. The Tortoise was saying, "Have you got that last step written down? Unless I've lost count, that makes a thousand and one. There are several millions more to come. And *would* you mind, as a personal favour, considering what a lot of instruction this colloquy of ours will provide for the Logicians of the Nineteenth Century—*would* you mind adopting a pun that my cousin the Mock-Turtle will then make, and allowing yourself to be re-named *Taught-Us?*"

"As you please!" replied the weary warrior, in the hollow tones of despair, as he buried his face in his hands. "Provided that *you*, for *your* part, will adopt a pun the Mock-Turtle never made, and allow yourself to be re-named *A Kill-Ease!*"

JOHN DEWEY

(1859-1952)

During a philosophical career (mostly at Columbia University) unusual in its length, productivity, and widespread influence, John Dewey returned repeatedly to the questions of logic. Indeed, some of the chief conceptions of his far-ranging philosophy are rooted and crowned in his logical theory. In Dewey the reciprocity between logic and metaphysics is less spectacular than in Russell, less rigorous than in Aristotle, less occult than in Mill, but no less genuine than in any.

Of primary significance is Dewey's persistent appeal to the uniqueness, the importance, the regulative activity of human ideas, confronting, in experimental success and failure, the spread of changing experience— what Dewey himself called the "pattern of inquiry." It is the full elaboration of this preoccupation with successful and unsuccessful experience that Dewey calls in the following sections "the instrumental theory," and which is known more popularly as "Pragmatism." Thus from its logical core Dewey's views emerge to a philosophy of experience itself, and, broader still, to a philosophy of the society of man and his institutions.

Accordingly, what is noteworthy, especially in the first of the following selections, is the way in which the view of the nature of logic, and the authority of its norms, is based upon nothing more commanding than the nature of experience—the latter being itself the experience of nature. Connected with this, and evident in both selections, is Dewey's profound philosophical and emotional distaste for immutable realities, and his inclination to see in the love of Being the root of all kinds of evils. This distaste is itself of course the reverse side of Dewey's own pragmatism, its rejection of all absolutes (also, it seems, in logic), and its renewed concern for the reorganization of experience.

Since the reorganization is most saliently marked for Dewey by its success and failure, it would seem that the broadest aim of logic would be to clarify and systematize what happens when the "pattern of inquiry" succeeds or fails. This view, slightly vague, slightly experimental, more than slightly challenging, emerges in the following selections in such a way as to make a discussion of logic continuous with a discussion of the theory of truth.

THE SIGNIFICANCE
OF LOGICAL RECONSTRUCTION[1]

Logic—like philosophy itself—suffers from a curious oscillation. It is elevated into the supreme and legislative science only to fall into the trivial estate of keeper of such statements as A is A and the scholastic verses for the syllogistic rules. It claims power to state the laws of the ultimate structure of the universe, on the ground that it deals with the laws of thought which are the laws according to which Reason has formed the world. Then it limits its pretensions to laws of correct reasoning which is correct even though it leads to no matter of fact, or even to material falsity. It is regarded by the modern objective idealist as the adequate substitute for ancient ontological metaphysics; but others treat it as that branch of rhetoric which teaches proficiency in argumentation. For a time a superficial compromise equilibrium was maintained wherein the logic of formal demonstration which the Middle Ages extracted from Aristotle was supplemented by an inductive logic of discovery of truth that Mill extracted from the practice of scientific men. But students of German philosophy, of mathematics, and of psychology, no matter how much they attacked one another, have made common cause in attack upon the orthodox logics both of deductive proof and inductive discovery.

Logical theory presents a scene of chaos. There is little agreement as to its subject-matter, scope or purpose. This disagreement is not formal or nominal but affects the treatment of every topic. Take such a rudimentary matter as the nature of judg-

---

[1] Reprinted from John Dewey, *Reconstruction in Philosophy* (New York: Holt, Rinehart and Winston, Inc., 1920).

ment. Reputable authority can be quoted in behalf of every possible permutation of doctrine. Judgment is the central thing in logic; and judgment is not logical at all, but personal and psychological. If logical, it is the primary function to which both conception and inference are subordinate; and it is an after-product from them. The distinction of subject and predicate is necessary, and it is totally irrelevant; or again, though it is found in some cases, it is not of great importance. Among those who hold that the subject-predicate relationship is essential, some hold that judgment is an analysis of something prior into them, and others assert that it is a synthesis of them into something else. Some hold that reality is always the subject of judgment, and others that "reality" is logically irrelevant. Among those who deny that judgment is the attribution of predicate to subject, who regard it as a relation of elements, some hold that the relation is "internal," some that it is "external," and others that it is sometimes one and sometimes the other.

Unless logic is a matter of some practical account, these contrarieties are so numerous, so extensive, and so irreconcilable that they are ludicrous. If logic is an affair of practical moment, then these inconsistencies are serious. They testify to some deeplying cause of intellectual disagreement and incoherency. In fact, contemporary logical theory is the ground upon which all philosophical differences and disputes are gathered together and focussed. How does the modification in the traditional conception of the relation of experience and reason, the real and ideal affect logic?

It affects, in the first place, the nature of logic itself. If thought or intelligence is the means of intentional reconstruction of experience, then logic, as an account of the procedure of thought, is not purely formal. It is not confined to laws of formally correct reasoning apart from truth of subject-matter. Neither, on the contrary, is it concerned with the inherent thought structures of the universe, as Hegel's logic would have it; nor with the successive approaches of human thought to this objective thought structure as the logic of Lotze, Bosanquet, and other epistemological logicians would have it. If thinking is the way in which deliberate reorganization of experience is secured, then logic is such a clarified and systematized formulation of the procedures of thinking as will enable the desired reconstruction to go on more economically and efficiently. In language familiar to students, logic is both a science and an art; a science so far as it gives an organized and tested descriptive account of the way in which thought actually goes on; an art, so far as on the basis of this description it projects methods by which future thinking shall take advantage of the operations that lead to success and avoid those which result in failure.

Thus is answered the dispute whether logic is empirical or normative, psychological or regulative. It is both. Logic is based on a definite and executive supply of empirical material. Men have been thinking for ages. They have observed, inferred, and reasoned in all sorts of ways and to all kinds of results. Anthropology, the study of the origin of myth, legend and cult; linguistics and grammar; rhetoric and former logical compositions all tell us how men have thought and what have been the purposes and consequences of different kinds of thinking. Psychology, experimental and pathological, makes important contributions to our knowledge of how thinking goes on and to what effect. Especially does the record of the growth of the various sciences afford instruction in those concrete ways of inquiry and testing which have led men astray and which have proved efficacious. Each science from mathematics to history exhibits typical fallacious methods and typical efficacious methods in special subject-matters. Logical theory has thus a large, almost inexhaustible field of empirical study.

The conventional statement that experience only tells us how men have thought or *do* think, while logic is concerned with norms, with how men *should* think, is ludicrously inept. Some sorts of thinking are shown *by* experience to have got nowhere, or worse than nowhere—into systematized delusion and mistake. Others have proved in manifest experience that they lead to fruitful and enduring discoveries. It is precisely in experience that the different consequences of different methods of investigation and ratiocination are convincingly shown. The parrot-like repetition of the distinction between an empirical description of what is and a normative account of what should be merely neglects the most striking fact about thinking as it empirically is—namely, its flagrant exhibition of cases of failure and success—that is, of good thinking and bad thinking. Any one who considers this empirical manifestation will not complain of lack of material from which to construct a *regulative* art. The more study that is given to empirical records of actual thought, the more apparent becomes the connection between the specific features of thinking which have produced failure and success. Out of this relationship of cause and effect as it is empirically ascertained grow the norms and regulations of an art of thinking.

Mathematics is often cited as an example of purely normative thinking dependent upon *a priori* canons and supra-empirical material. But it is hard to see how the student who approaches the matter historically can avoid the conclusion that the status of mathematics is as empirical as that of metallurgy. Men began with counting and measuring things just as they began with pounding and burning them. One thing, as common speech profoundly has it, led to another. Certain ways were successful —not merely in the immediately practical sense, but in the sense of being interesting, of arousing attention, of exciting attempts at improvement. The present-day mathematical logician may present the structure of mathematics as if it had sprung all at once from the brain of a Zeus whose anatomy is that of pure logic. But, nevertheless, this very structure is a product of long historic growth, in which all kinds of experiments have been tried, in which some men have struck out in this direction and some in that, and in which some exercises and operations have resulted in confusion and others in triumphant clarifications and fruitful growths; a history in which matter and methods have been constantly selected and worked over on the basis of empirical success and failure.

The structure of alleged normative *a priori* mathematics is in truth the crowned result of ages of toilsome experience. The metallurgist who should write on the most highly developed method of dealing with ores would not, in truth, proceed any differently. He too selects, refines, and organizes the methods which in the past have been found to yield the maximum of achievement. Logic is a matter of profound human importance precisely because it is empirically founded and experimentally applied. So considered, the problem of logical theory is none other than the problem of the possibility of the development and employment of intelligent method in inquiries concerned with deliberate reconstruction of experience.

*   *   *

That which is not already in existence, that which is only anticipated and inferred, cannot be observed. It does not have the status of fact, of something given, a datum, but of a meaning, an idea. So far as ideas are not fancies, framed by emotionalized memory for escape and refuge, they are precisely anticipations of something still to come aroused by looking into the facts of a developing situation. The blacksmith watches his iron, its color and texture, to get evidence of what it is getting ready to pass into; the physician observes his patient to detect symptoms of change in some definite direction; the scientific man keeps his attention upon his laboratory material to get a clue as to what *will* happen under certain conditions. The very fact that observation is not an end in itself but a search for evidence and signs shows that along with observation goes inference, anticipatory forecast—in short an idea, thought or conception.

In a more technical context, it would be worth while to see what light this logical correspondence of observed fact and projected idea or meaning throws upon certain traditional philosophical problems and puzzles, including that of subject and predicate in judgment, object and subject in knowledge, "real" and "ideal" generally. But at this time, we must confine ourselves to pointing out that this view of the correlative origin and function of observed fact and projected idea in experience, commits us to some very important consequences concerning the nature of ideas, meanings, conceptions, or whatever word may be employed to denote the specifically *mental* function. Because they are suggestions of something that may happen or eventuate, they are (as we saw in the case of ideals generally) platforms of response to what is going on. The man who detects that the cause of his difficulty is an automobile bearing down upon him is not guaranteed safety; he may have made his observation-forecast too late. But if his anticipation-perception comes in season, he has the basis for doing something which will avert threatening disaster. Because he foresees an impending result, he may do something that will lead to the situation eventuating in some other way. All intelligent thinking means an increment of freedom in action—an emancipation from chance and fatality. "Thought" represents the suggestion of a way of response that is different from that which would have been followed if intelligent observation had not effected an inference as to the future.

*   *   *

As the instrumental theory is favorable to high esteem for impartial and disinterested inquiry, so, contrary to the impressions of some critics, it sets much store upon the apparatus of deduction. It is a strange notion that because one says that the cognitive value of conceptions, definitions, generalizations, classifications and the development of consecutive implications is not self-resident, that therefore one makes light of the deductive function, or denies its fruitfulness and necessity. The instrumental theory only attempts to state with some scrupulousness *where* the value is found and to prevent its being sought in the wrong place. It says that knowing begins with specific observations that define the problem and ends with specific observations that test a hypothesis for its solution. But that the idea, the meaning, which the original observations suggest and the final ones test, itself requires careful scrutiny and prolonged development, the theory would be the last to deny. To say that a locomotive is an agency, that it is intermediate between a need in experience and its satisfaction, is not to depreciate the worth of careful and elaborate construction of the locomotive, or the need of subsidiary tools and processes that are devoted to introducing improvements into its structure. One would rather say that *because* the locomotive is intermediary in experience, not primary and not final, it is impossible to devote too much care to its constructive development.

Such a deductive science as mathematics represents the perfecting of method. That a method to those concerned with it should present itself as an end on its own account is no more surprising than that there should be a distinct business for making any tool. Rarely are those who invent and perfect a tool those who employ it. There is, indeed, one marked difference between the physical and the intellectual instrumentality. The development of the latter runs far beyond any immediately visible use. The artistic interest in perfecting the method by itself is strong—as the utensils of civilization may themselves become works of finest art. But from the practical standpoint this difference shows that the advantage as an instrumentality is on the side of the intellectual tool. Just because it is not formed with a special application in mind, because it is a highly generalized tool, it is the more flexible in adaptation to unforeseen uses. It can be employed in dealing with problems that were not anticipated. The mind is prepared in advance for all sorts of intellectual emergencies, and when the new problem occurs it does not have to wait till it can get a special instrument ready.

More definitely, abstraction is indispensable if one experience is to be applicable in other experiences. Every concrete experience in its totality is unique; it is itself, non-reduplicable. Taken in its full concreteness, it yields no instruction, it throws no light. What is called abstraction means that some phase of it is selected for the sake of the aid it gives in grasping something else. Taken by itself, it is a mangled fragment, a poor substitute for the living whole from which it is extracted. But viewed teleologically or practically, it represents the only way in which one experience can be made of any value for another —the only way in which something enlightening can be secured. What is called false or vicious abstractionism signifies that the *function* of the detached fragment is forgotten and neglected, so that it is esteemed barely in itself as something of a higher order than the muddy and irregular concrete from which it was wrenched. Looked at functionally, not structurally and statically, abstraction means that something has been released from one experience for transfer to another. Abstraction is liberation. The more theoretical, the more abstract, an abstraction, or the farther away it is from anything experienced in its concreteness, the better fitted it is to deal with any one of the indefinite variety of things that may later present themselves. Ancient mathematics and physics were much nearer the gross concrete experience than are modern. For that very reason they were more impotent in affording any insight into and control over such concretes as present themselves in new and unexpected forms.

Abstraction and generalization have always been recognized as close kin. It may be said that they are the negative and positive sides of the same function. Abstraction sets free some factor so that it may be used. Generalization is the use. It carries over and extends. It is always in some sense a leap in the dark. It is an adventure. There can be no assurance in advance that what is extracted from one concrete can be fruitfully extended to another individual case. Since these other cases are individual and concrete they *must* be dissimilar. The trait of flying is detached from the concrete bird. This abstraction is then carried over to the bat, and it is expected in view of the application of the quality to have some of the other traits of the bird. This trivial instance indicates the essence of generalization, and also illustrates the riskiness of the proceeding. It transfers, extends, applies, a result of some former experience to the reception and interpretation of a new one. Deductive processes define, delimit, purify and set in order the conceptions through which this enriching and directive operation is carried on, but they cannot, however perfect, guarantee the outcome.

*   *   *

Little time is left to speak of the account of the nature of truth given by the experimental and functional type of logic. This is less to be regretted because this account is completely a corollary from the nature of thinking and ideas. If the view held as to the latter is understood, the conception of truth follows as a matter of course. If it be not understood, any attempt to present the theory of truth is bound to be confusing, and the theory itself to seem arbitrary and absurd. *If* ideas, meanings, conceptions, notions, theories, systems are instrumental to an active reorganization of the given environment, to a removal of some specific trouble and perplexity, then the test of their validity and value lies in accomplishing this work. If they succeed in their office, they are reliable, sound, valid, good, true. If they fail to clear up confusion, to eliminate defects, if they increase confusion, uncertainty and evil when they are acted upon, then are they false. Confirmation, corroboration, verification lie in works, consequences. Handsome is that handsome does. By their fruits shall ye *know* them. That which guides us truly is true— demonstrated capacity for such guidance is precisely what is meant by truth. The adverb "truly" is more fundamental than either the adjective, true, or the noun, truth. An adverb expresses a way, a mode of acting. Now an idea or conception is a claim or injunction or plan to *act* in a certain way as the way to arrive at the clearing up of a specific situation. When the claim or pretension or plan is acted upon *it guides us truly or falsely;* it leads us to our end or away from it. Its active, dynamic function is the all-important thing about it, and in the quality of activity induced by it lies all its truth and falsity. The hypothesis that works is the *true* one; and *truth* is an abstract noun applied to the collection of cases, actual, foreseen and desired, that receive confirmation in their works and consequences.

So wholly does the worth of this conception of truth depend upon the correctness of the prior account of thinking that it is more profitable to consider why the conception gives offence than to expound it on its own account. Part of the reason why it has been found so obnoxious is doubtless its novelty and defects in its statement. Too often, for example, when truth has been thought of as satisfaction, it has been thought of as merely emotional satisfaction, a private comfort, a meeting of purely personal need. But the satisfaction in question means a satisfaction of the needs and conditions of the problem out of which the idea, the purpose and method of action, arises. It includes public and objective conditions. It is not to be manipulated by whim or personal idiosyncrasy. Again when truth is defined as utility, it is often thought to mean utility for some purely personal end, some profit upon which a particular individual has set his heart. So repulsive is a conception of truth which makes it a mere tool of private ambition and aggrandizement, that the wonder is that critics have attributed such a notion to sane men. As matter of fact, truth as utility means service in making just that contribution to reorganization in experience that the idea or theory claims to be able to make. The usefulness of a road is not measured by the degree in which it lends itself to the purposes of a highwayman. It is measured by whether it actually functions *as* a road, as a means of easy and effective public transportation and communication. And so with the serviceableness of an idea or hypothesis as a measure of its truth.

Turning from such rather superficial misunderstandings, we find, I think, the chief obstacle to the reception of this notion of truth in an inheritance from the classic tradition that has become so deeply engrained in men's minds. In just the degree in which existence is divided into two realms, a higher one of perfect being and a lower one of seeming, phenomenal, deficient reality, truth and falsity are thought of as fixed, ready-made static properties of things themselves. Supreme Reality is true Being, inferior and imperfect Reality is false Being. It makes claims to Reality which it cannot substantiate. It is deceitful, fraudulent, inherently unworthy of trust and belief. Beliefs are false not because they mislead us; they are not mistaken ways of thinking. They are false because they admit and adhere to false existences or subsistences. Other notions are true because they do have to do with true Being—with full and ultimate Reality. Such a notion lies at the back of the head of every one who has, in however an indirect way, been a recipient of the ancient and medieval tradition. This view is radically challenged by the pragmatic conception of truth, and the impossibility of reconciliation or compromise is, I think, the cause of the shock occasioned by the newer theory.

This contrast, however, constitutes the importance of the new theory as well as the unconscious obstruction to its acceptance. The older conception worked out practically to identify truth with authoritative dogma. A society that chiefly esteems order, that finds growth painful and change disturbing, inevitably seeks for a fixed body of superior truths upon which it may depend. It looks backward, to something already in existence, for the source and sanction of truth. It falls back upon what is antecedent, prior, original, *a priori,* for assurance. The thought of looking ahead, toward the eventual, toward consequences, creates uneasiness and fear. It disturbs the sense of rest that is attached to the ideas of fixed Truth already in existence. It puts a heavy burden of responsibility upon us for search, unremitting observation, scrupulous development of hypotheses and thoroughgoing testing. In physical matters men have slowly grown accustomed in all specific beliefs to identifying the true with the verified. But they still hesitate to recognize the implication of this identification and to derive the definition of truth from it. For while it is nominally agreed upon as a commonplace that definitions ought to spring from concrete and specific cases rather than be invented in the empty air and imposed upon particulars, there is a strange unwillingness to act upon the maxim in defining truth. To generalize the recognition that the true means the verified and means nothing else places upon men the responsibility for surrendering political and moral dogmas, and subjecting to the test of consequences their most cherished prejudices. Such a change involves a great change in the seat of authority and the methods of decision in society.

*   *   *

INDUCTION AND DEDUCTION[1]

Whatever else scientific method is or is not, it is concerned with ascertaining the conjunctions of characteristic traits which descriptively determine kinds in relation to one another, and with the interrelations of characters constituting abstract conceptions of wide applicability. The propositions which result are generalizations of two forms, generic and universal; one existential in content, the other non-existential. The methods by which generalizations are arrived at have received the name "induction"; the methods by which already existing generalizations are employed have received the name "deduction." These considerations at least delimit the field of discussion. Any account of scientific method must be capable of offering a coherent doctrine of the nature of induction and deduction and of their relations to one another and the doctrine must accord with what takes place in actual scientific practice.

With respect to both induction and deduction, the logical terrain is still occupied with remnants, some more or less coherent and some more or less of the nature of debris, of logical conceptions that were formed prior to the development of scientific method. There is, accordingly, no field of logical subject-matter in which the need of thoroughgoing reform of theory is as urgent as in the case of induction and deduction. It has become traditional to repeat the statements that induction goes from particulars to the general and deduction from the general to the particulars. The extent to which these conceptions are valid, i.e., in harmony with scientific practice, is not critically examined. The result too frequently is that actual scientific

---

[1] Reprinted from John Dewey, *Logic: The Theory of Inquiry* (New York: Holt, Rinehart and Winston, Inc., 1938).

procedure is forced into the strait-jacket of irrelevant preconceptions. Escape from this procedure depends upon analyses of induction and deduction from the point of view of method as exhibited in actual methods of inquiry.

The traditional and still current conceptions of induction and deduction are derived from Aristotelian logic, which, as has been shown, was a systematization of logical forms on the basis of certain cosmological beliefs. Since the actual progress of scientific inquiry has led to an abandonment of these underlying beliefs concerning the structure of Nature, it might be antecedently expected that the doctrines about induction and deduction which are found in the Aristotelian logic, will be so irrelevant to existing scientific practice as to be the source of confusion and uncertainty when they are employed as rubrics of interpretation.

A. *Induction and Deduction in Aristotelian Logic.* The conception of induction as a procedure that goes from particulars to the general, and of deduction as the reverse movement, has its origin in the Aristotelian formulation. More important than the mere question of its historical derivation is the fact that the Aristotelian conceptions were relevant to, and grounded in, the subject-matter of natural science *as that subject-matter, the structure of nature, was then understood.* There is no need at this point to expound at length the characteristic features of the conception of nature entertained by Aristotle. The distinction between immutable Being, existing at all times in identical form, and the mutable, which in its mutability is convincing proof of partial and incomplete Being provided the ground of the distinction made between induction and rationally complete, scientific demonstration or deduction. Since the immutable was constituted by fixed species, each of which was defined by an essence, it followed that strictly scientific or demonstrative knowledge consisted in a classificatory ordering of fixed species, in which inclusive species hierarchically determined included species of a more limited range. This ordering is effected in the demonstrative syllogism. Scientific knowledge of changing things is, on the contrary, possible only when and as these things are caught and placed within the fixed limits constituted by essences that define species. The result here was also expressed in the syllogism, but in a contingent syllogism as distinct from the rational necessity of the demonstrative syllogism.[2]

In each of these forms, the deductive is identified with the syllogistic. Given the underlying cosmological assumptions, there is genuine meaning in the conception of going from the general to the more particular. In the case of the demonstrative syllogism, the movement is from the more to the less inclusive. Where "particular" is to be understood in a strictly logical sense—as equivalent to the more specific in its distinction from the universal inclusive species. In the case of the contingent syllogism, "particular" has a different meaning. Anything which is mutable is particular in the sense of being partial, incomplete. Now the objects of sense perception are observed things in their severalty in distinction from the species to which they belong. They are, as just noted, truly known only when and as they are subsumed under universal propositions, which state the inherent nature of species. As thus subsumed, they "follow" as particulars from the general.

At this point, I shall briefly indicate the difference between this conception of rational demonstration and that which is in accord with present scientific practice. Mathematical discourse is now the outstanding exemplar of deductive demonstration; but (i) no mathematician would regard it as logically important to reduce a chain of related mathematical propositions to the syllogistic form, nor would he suppose that such reduction added anything to the force of his demonstration; and (ii) such deductions *do not* necessarily proceed from the more general to the less general even with respect to conceptions: while (iii) (as is generally acknowledged), it is impossible to proceed directly from a universal proposition to one about an existential particular or singular. It is true (with regard to the second point) that sometimes in mathematical reasoning the final proposition

---

[2] To express the contingent nature of this form of syllogism, Aristotle frequently uses the expression "dialectic syllogisms." Their conclusions are true as a rule, "upon the whole," usually, but not always, since they are not derived from subject-matters which are themselves necessary.

has less scope or "comprehension," a narrower range of applicability, than do the preceding propositions from which it "follows." When, for example, an ellipse is defined as a curve so moving that its distance from a fixed line bears a constant ratio to its distance from a fixed point, the logical movement is from a conception of wider applicability to one restricted by introduction of a special limiting condition. But when the properties of an ellipse are defined by reasoning from the properties of a conic section, the logical movement is from the narrower to the wider range of applicability. When the equilateral is derived from the equiangular, there is neither gain nor loss in comprehension or scope. The fact is that about mathematical reasoning, as an example of deduction, no general statement whatever can be made as to the breadth of the premises in relation to that of the conclusion. Such differences as may be present depend upon the special methods used and the nature of the problem dealt with. So much, in general, for the irrelevancy of the Aristotelian conception of deduction to modern scientific practice.

With respect to the formulation of the inductive procedures of ancient and modern science respectively, there exists a verbal similarity. Both start from scattered data (or particulars) and move toward institution of generalizations. But the similarity does not extend beyond the vague formula of "going from particulars to generals." For (a) particulars are conceived in radically different ways and (b) the process of "going," or the way in which generals are arrived at from particulars, is very different. A survey of the Aristotelian conception of induction suffices to show its intrinsic unfitness to serve the logical conditions of present science. The cosmological theory of Aristotle postulates that every knowable thing is of some kind or species. Even sense-perception is a mode of low-grade knowledge in so far as what is seen, heard and touched is apprehended as being of a kind. The very lowest grade of knowledge, mere sensation, directly apprehends qualities determined by "sensible forms," such as, in touch, hard or soft. Sensation and sense-perception are modes of knowledge in which "matter," the principle of change and hence of lack of Being, predominates, as, *e.g.,* when the dry changes to the wet. In general, the "particular" which is "known" in sense perception is subject to generation and dissolution, to "birth" and "death," as a tree grows from seed, decays and vanishes. *Recurrent* perceptions then constitute experience. In persons who are happily constituted by natural endowment, who have the scientific and philosophic *nisus* or potentiality, the form is gradually apprehended *as such,* first as subduing matter, and then finally as completely free from any connection with matter. Definition and classification are thus instituted and there is scientific knowledge on the basis of rational apprehension or notation. In short, the universal is grasped in its own inherent nature. This process constitutes in the classic scheme the "going" from particulars to the universal which is induction. "Forms" which are immutable, necessary and universal, are present from the first in qualities and objects of sensation and sense perception. Induction is but the process by which these forms are so *elicited* from entanglement in "matter" that they are perceived by reason in their own essential nature, "reason" being defined precisely as this actualization in knowledge of pure forms of Being.

"Induction" on this basis is a psychological process, although not in the subjective sense of psychological which has controlled so much of modern speculation. The process in question is rather biological, and the biological is an actualization of the cosmological. It is, accordingly, perhaps better to think of it as a *pedagogical* process in which certain select persons in whom the potentiality of reason is brought to actuality by means of the forms that are implicit in objects of experience, are *led up to* or *induced* to apprehend universals which have been necessarily involved, all the time, in sense qualities and objects of empirical perception. *Epagoge,* the word translated by our word "induction," is then precisely the process of being *led or brought up to* apprehension of fixed and essential forms in and of themselves.

B. *The Nature of Induction on the Ground of Prior Analyses.* I shall give a brief *formal* statement of its nature in the light of previous discussion. (i) Particulars are *selectively* discriminated

so as to determine a *problem* whose nature is such as to indicate
possible modes of solution. This selective redetermination of
perceived objects and their qualities necessarily involves experimental transformation of objects and qualities in their given
"natural" state, whereas in the classic logic they were taken "as
is." (ii) The particulars of observations which are experimentally instituted not only form the subject-matter of a *problem* so
as to indicate an appropriate mode of solution, but are also
such as to have *evidential and testing* value with respect to indicated modes of solution. Operations are deliberately performed that experimentally modify given antecedent objects of
perception, so as to produce *new* data in new ordered arrangement. Institution of new data which are relevant and effective
with respect to any conclusion that is hypothetically entertained,
forms the most indispensable and difficult part of inquiry in the
natural sciences. Objects and qualities as they naturally present
themselves or as they are "given," are not only *not* the data of
science, but they constitute the most direct and important obstacle to formation of those ideas and hypotheses that are genuinely relevant and effective.

The primary meanings and associations of ideas and hypotheses are derived from their position and force in common sense
situations of use-enjoyment. They are expressed in symbols
developed originally for the sake of social communication rather
than to serve the conditions of controlled inquiry. The symbols
are therefore loaded with meanings that are irrelevant to inquiry conducted for the sake of attaining knowledge as such.
These meanings are familiar and influentially persuasive because of their established associations. The result is that the
historic advance of science is marked and accompanied by deliberate elimination of such terms and institution in their
stead of a new set of symbols constituting a new technical language. The progress of every science—physics, chemistry, biol-
ogy, and even mathematics—in general and in particular, is
evidence both of the difficulty and necessity of instituting data
of a new order.

What is the analysis of those scientific procedures to which the name induction may be applied if the word has any application at all? For the question is not about the meaning of a word, even of a word that has been sanctioned by long usage, but of the actual procedures by which generalizations are established in the natural sciences. Moreover, generalizations are of two forms. There are those which institute a relation of including and included kinds, and there are those which institute universal *if-then* propositions as hypotheses and theories. Any adequate account of scientific methods as the means by which warranted generalizations are achieved must, therefore, be applicable to both of these two forms. This consideration is, in effect, a warning in advance of the impossibility of making a sharp division between "induction" as the operation by which *existential* generalizations are established, and "deduction" as the operation concerned with the relations of universal propositions in discourse. As far as physical inquiry, at least, is concerned, induction and deduction must be so interpreted that they will be seen to be coöperative phases of the same ultimate set of operations.

This is a summary statement of conclusions regarding the distinctively inductive and deductive phases of inquiry, and their interrelation, or functional correspondence, with each other. (a) The inductive phase consists of the complex of experimental operations by which antecedently existing conditions are so modified that data are obtained which indicate and test proposed modes of solution. (b) Any suggested or indicated mode of solution must be formulated as a *possibility*. Such formulation constitutes a hypothesis. The *if-then* proposition which results must be developed in ordered relation to other propositions of like form (or in discourse), until related contents are obtained forming the special *if-then* proposition that directs experimental observations yielding new data. The criterion for the validity of such hypotheses is the capacity of the new data they produce to combine with earlier data (describing the problem) so that they institute a whole of unified significance. (c) The nature of the interrelation or functional correspondence of these two phases of inquiry directly follows. The propositions which formulate data must, to satisfy the conditions of inquiry, be such as to determine a problem in the form that indicates a possible solution, while the hypothesis in which the latter is formulated must be such as operationally to provide the new data that fill out and order those previously obtained. There is a continued to and fro movement between the set of existential propositions about data and the non-existential propositions about related conceptions.

This formulation agrees up to a certain point with current statements about scientific inquiry as *hypothetical-deductive* in nature. But it emphasizes two necessary conditions which are usually slurred in statement of that position: (a) The necessity of observational determinations in order to indicate a relevant hypothesis, and (b) the necessity of *existential* operational application of the hypothesis in order to institute existential material capable of testing the hypothesis. These conditions place the hypothetical-deductive stage of inquiry as intermediate. When this stage is taken in isolation from the initial and terminal stages of inquiry (concerned with existential observations), it is disconnected from its occasion in problems, and from its application in their solution. It is probable that in the current formulation of the position, these stages are taken for granted or are "understood." But it is necessary to state them explicitly in order that the hypothetical-deductive stage may be relevant and controlled in its contents and their order of relation. Otherwise it is assumed (a) that existential propositions are "implied" by universal propositions, and (b) that affirming the antecedent when and because the consequent is affirmed, is valid.

The conjugate relation of the inductive and deductive is exemplified in the correlative nature of inference and proof, where "proof" means ostensive demonstration. That it is highly uneconomical from the practical point of view to separate the two functions of inference and test is clear without extensive argument. Economy makes it important that the material *from* which an inference is drawn should also be such as far as is possible to test the inference that is made. For it is important that the inference drawn should be such as to indicate *what* new kinds of data are required and give some suggestion as to *how* they are to be obtained. But the importance of including within one and the same set of methodic procedures, operations that produce material which is both evidentially indicative, testing and testable, is much more than a matter of practical economy. It is logically necessary. For an "inference" that is not *grounded* in the evidential nature of the material from which it is drawn is *not* an inference. It is a more or less wild guess. To say that an inference is *grounded* in any degree whatever is equivalent to saying that the material upon which it is based is such as to be a factor in warranting its validity: not in its isolation, but in connection with the new data obtained as consequences of the operations to which the inference, as a hypothesis, led. The progress made by inquiry in any branch may, then, be measured by the extent to which it has succeeded in developing methods of inquiry that, at one and the same time, provide material data having conjunct inferential and testing force. *Satisfaction of this condition provides the definition of inductive procedures.*

Uncritical adherence to Aristotelian conceptions has combined with the prestige of physics, especially of mathematical physics, to generate the conception that physics is not only the *most* advanced form of scientific inquiry (which it undeniably is), but that it is *alone* scientific in nature. From a popular standpoint, application of physical generalizations, as in the technologies of the electric and chemical engineer and in the methods used by "medical science" (if the term be allowed) appeal chiefly because of their practical consequences. But from a logical standpoint the applications are integral parts of the verification of the generalizations themselves. The drainage of swamps where anopheles mosquitoes breed is prized because it helps to eliminate malaria. But from the scientific standpoint it is an experiment which confirms a theory. In general, wide social application of the results of physics and chemistry provides added test and security for conclusions reached.

The issue involved is a far-reaching one. Dogmatic restriction of science to generalizations compels denial of scientific traits and value to every form of practice. It obliterates, logically, the enormous difference that exists between activities that are routine and those that are intelligent; between action dictated by caprice and the conduct of arts that embody technologies and techniques expressing systematically tested ideas. Even more to the point is the fact that it involves logical suicide of the sciences with respect even to generalizations. For there is no ground whatever upon which a logical line can be drawn between the operations and techniques of experimentation in the natural sciences and the same operations and techniques employed for distinctively practical ends. Nothing so fatal to science can be imagined as elimination of experimentation, and experimentation is a form of doing and making. Application of conceptions and hypotheses to existential matters through the medium of doing and making is an intrinsic constituent of scientific method. No hard and fast line can be drawn between such forms of "practical" activity and those which apply *their* conclusions to human social ends without involving disastrous consequences to science in its narrower sense.

BERTRAND RUSSELL

Born in 1872, he was elected Fellow of the Royal Society in 1908, succeeded to the earldom in 1931, received the Order of Merit in 1949, and was given the Nobel Prize for Literature in 1950.

The philosophical influence of Bertrand Russell, much of it now at second and third hand, is probably greater than that of any other English speaking philosopher of this century. Next to him stands Ludwig Wittgenstein, first a powerful and independent ally, then an equally powerful and independent critic. One thinks of the celebrated remark of one of their colleagues: "It is well known that Wittgenstein has never written a philosophy and that Bertrand Russell writes a new one every year." On logic, however, Russell's views exhibit less vacillation. Here, his work, and that of his forerunners and disciples, has gradually but surely transformed the entire subject. It is, to name but one instance, more because of Russell than of any other, that almost every university now offers courses in symbolic (or mathematical) logic. The actual nature of the transformation, however, is an extraordinarily complicated and technical affair, impossible to characterize in one page or to capture in one book. So let us attempt it in three sentences, one abstract, one concrete, one illustrative.

Boole and De Morgan, English contemporaries of John Stuart Mill, had developed, with others, a symbolic logic which included Aristotle, more or less—more technical finesse, less metaphysical finery; drawing on the Italian G. Peano and the German G. Frege, Russell not only consolidated all these results but brought the subject to far wider attention and importance by relating mathematics to logic. Concretely, Russell offered precise and frequently novel definitions and sometimes new notations for such ideas as *class, member of, implies, the, relation,* and *every;* he combined these with a few primitive axioms and auxiliary principles, and then demonstrated (with the help of Whitehead) that we can, with these so-called "logical ideas," deduce the whole of mathematics. Illustratively, Russell defined *one* as: "the number of a class u such that there is a term x, belonging to u, such that 'y is a u and y differs from x' is always false"

111

(*The Principles of Mathematics,* p. 356), and then sought to account for all the assumptions of the definition.

All this is a suitable subject to pursue after the present one has been mastered. Meanwhile there is the reflecting upon some of the reverberations of the new logic. In this respect Russell's innovations inspired him to a bold contempt for what went before. Mainly what went before Russell (and, to his profound disgust, what goes after) is Aristotle. Like the rest of us, Russell's capacity for understanding his antagonists is not improved by a strongly polemical stance; so the ensuing pages will bear watching for one-sidedness. But not for that are they here presented. Rather, because we have here a challenging telescopic view of the logical landscape exhibited by one who has himself redrawn the map.

The first selection, "On Induction," was written about the same time that Russell was making his major contribution, mentioned above, to deductive logic. There is, however, no such obvious connection between his theories on induction and deduction as there was for Mill. This essay, though, is an early statement of Russell; he offered a much elaborated theory of induction almost forty years later (*Human Knowledge: Its Scope and Limits*). The next essay, "Logic as the Essence of Philosophy," shows some uncertainty as to whether induction qualifies as logic; but it exhibits a philosophical side of the new logic and nicely illustrates its thesis that while "the old logic put thought in fetters . . . the new logic gives it wings." The wings have since then taken Russell on other philosophical flights, and he has not continued to uphold all the special metaphysical theses which are to be found in this essay. The third selection on "Aristotle's Logic" shows Russell in partisan array, arguing in effect that those who reject his logic are not only reactionary but birds of a fetter.

ON INDUCTION[1]

*   *   *

What things are there in the universe whose existence is known to us owing to our being acquainted with them? So far,

---

[1] Reprinted from Bertrand Russell, *The Problems of Philosophy* (London: Oxford University Press, 1912). By permission.

our answer has been that we are acquainted with our sense-data, and, probably, with ourselves. These we know to exist. And past sense-data which are remembered are known to have existed in the past. This knowledge supplies our data.

But if we are to be able to draw inferences from these data— if we are to know of the existence of matter, of other people, of the past before our individual memory begins, or of the future, we must know general principles of some kind by means of which such inferences can be drawn. It must be known to us that the existence of some one sort of thing, A, is a sign of the existence of some other sort of thing, B, either at the same time as A or at some earlier or later time, as, for example, thunder is a sign of the earlier existence of lightning. If this were not known to us, we could never extend our knowledge beyond the sphere of our private experience; and this sphere, as we have seen, is exceedingly limited. The question we have now to consider is whether such an extension is possible, and if so, how it is effected.

Let us take as an illustration a matter about which none of us, in fact, feel the slightest doubt. We are all convinced that the sun will rise to-morrow. Why? Is this belief a mere blind outcome of past experience, or can it be justified as a reasonable belief? It is not easy to find a test by which to judge whether a belief of this kind is reasonable or not, but we can at least ascertain what sort of general beliefs would suffice, if true, to justify the judgement that the sun will rise to-morrow, and the many other similar judgements upon which our actions are based.

It is obvious that if we are asked why we believe that the sun will rise to-morrow, we shall naturally answer, 'Because it always has risen every day.' We have a firm belief that it will rise in the future, because it has risen in the past. If we are challenged as to why we believe that it will continue to rise as heretofore, we may appeal to the laws of motion: the earth, we shall say, is a freely rotating body, and such bodies do not cease to rotate unless something interferes from outside, and there is nothing outside to interfere with the earth between now and

to-morrow. Of course it might be doubted whether we are quite
certain that there is nothing outside to interfere, but this is not
the interesting doubt. The interesting doubt is as to whether
the laws of motion will remain in operation until to-morrow. If
this doubt is raised, we find ourselves in the same position as
when the doubt about the sunrise was first raised.

The *only* reason for believing that the laws of motion will remain in operation is that they have operated hitherto, so far as
our knowledge of the past enables us to judge. It is true that we
have a greater body of evidence from the past in favour of the
laws of motion than we have in favour of the sunrise, because
the sunrise is merely a particular case of fulfilment of the laws
of motion, and there are countless other particular cases. But
the real question is: Do *any* number of cases of a law being fulfilled in the past afford evidence that it will be fulfilled in the
future? If not, it becomes plain that we have no ground whatever for expecting the sun to rise to-morrow, or for expecting
the bread we shall eat at our next meal not to poison us, or for
any of the other scarcely conscious expectations that control our
daily lives. It is to be observed that all such expectations are only
probable; thus we have not to seek for a proof that they *must* be
fulfilled, but only for some reason in favour of the view that they
are *likely* to be fulfilled.

Now in dealing with this question we must, to begin with,
make an important distinction, without which we should soon
become involved in hopeless confusions. Experience has shown
us that, hitherto, the frequent repetition of some uniform succession or coexistence has been a *cause* of our expecting the same
succession or coexistence on the next occasion. Food that has a
certain appearance generally has a certain taste, and it is a severe
shock to our expectations when the familiar appearance is found
to be associated with an unusual taste. Things which we see become associated, by habit, with certain tactile sensations which
we expect if we touch them; one of the horrors of a ghost (in
many ghost-stories) is that it fails to give us any sensations of
touch. Uneducated people who go abroad for the first time are

so surprised as to be incredulous when they find their native language not understood.

And this kind of association is not confined to men; in animals also it is very strong. A horse which has been often driven along a certain road resists the attempt to drive him in a different direction. Domestic animals expect food when they see the person who usually feeds them. We know that all these rather crude expectations of uniformity are liable to be misleading. The man who has fed the chicken every day throughout its life at last wrings its neck instead, showing that more refined views as to the uniformity of nature would have been useful to the chicken.

But in spite of the misleadingness of such expectations, they nevertheless exist. The mere fact that something has happened a certain number of times causes animals and men to expect that it will happen again. Thus our instincts certainly cause us to believe that the sun will rise to-morrow, but we may be in no better a position than the chicken which unexpectedly has its neck wrung. We have therefore to distinguish the fact that past uniformities *cause* expectations as to the future, from the question whether there is any reasonable ground for giving weight to such expectations after the question of their validity has been raised.

The problem we have to discuss is whether there is any reason for believing in what is called 'the uniformity of nature.' The belief in the uniformity of nature is the belief that everything that has happened or will happen is an instance of some general law to which there are *no* exceptions. The crude expectations which we have been considering are all subject to exceptions, and therefore liable to disappoint those who entertain them. But science habitually assumes, at least as a working hypothesis, that general rules which have exceptions can be replaced by general rules which have no exceptions. 'Unsupported bodies in air fall' is a general rule to which balloons and aeroplanes are exceptions. But the laws of motion and the law of gravitation, which account for the fact that most bodies fall, also account for the fact that balloons and aeroplanes can rise; thus the laws of motion and the law of gravitation are not subject to these exceptions.

The belief that the sun will rise to-morrow might be falsified if the earth came suddenly into contact with a large body which destroyed its rotation; but the laws of motion and the law of gravitation would not be infringed by such an event. The business of science is to find uniformities, such as the laws of motion and the law of gravitation, to which, so far as our experience extends, there are no exceptions. In this search science has been remarkably successful, and it may be conceded that such uniformities have held hitherto. This brings us back to the question: Have we any reason, assuming that they have always held in the past, to suppose that they will hold in the future?

It has been argued that we have reason to know that the future will resemble the past, because what was the future has constantly become the past, and has always been found to resemble the past, so that we really have experience of the future, namely of times which were formerly future, which we may call past futures. But such an argument really begs the very question at issue. We have experience of past futures, but not of future futures, and the question is: Will future futures resemble past futures? This question is not to be answered by an argument which starts from past futures alone. We have therefore still to seek for some principle which shall enable us to know that the future will follow the same laws as the past.

The reference to the future in this question is not essential. The same question arises when we apply the laws that work in our experience to past things of which we have no experience—as, for example, in geology, or in theories as to the origin of the Solar System. The question we really have to ask is: 'When two things have been found to be often associated, and no instance is known of the one occurring without the other, does the occurrence of one of the two, in a fresh instance, give any good ground for expecting the other?' On our answer to this question must depend the validity of the whole of our expectations as to the future, the whole of the results obtained by induction, and in fact practically all the beliefs upon which our daily life is based.

It must be conceded, to begin with, that the fact that two things have been found often together and never apart does not, by itself, suffice to *prove* demonstratively that they will be found together in the next case we examine. The most we can hope is that the oftener things are found together, the more probable it becomes that they will be found together another time, and that, if they have been found together often enough, the probability will amount *almost* to certainty. It can never quite reach certainty, because we know that in spite of frequent repetitions there sometimes is a failure at the last, as in the case of the chicken whose neck is wrung. Thus probability is all we ought to seek.

It might be urged, as against the view we are advocating, that we know all natural phenomena to be subject to the reign of law, and that sometimes, on the basis of observation, we can see that only one law can possibly fit the facts of the case. Now to this view there are two answers. The first is that, even if *some* law which has no exceptions applies to our case, we can never, in practice, be sure that we have discovered that law and not one to which there are exceptions. The second is that the reign of law would seem to be itself only probable, and that our belief that it will hold in the future, or in unexamined cases in the past, is itself based upon the very principle we are examining.

The principle we are examining may be called the *principle of induction,* and its two parts may be stated as follows:

(*a*) When a thing of a certain sort A has been found to be associated with a thing of a certain other sort B, and has never been found dissociated from a thing of the sort B, the greater the number of cases in which A and B have been associated, the greater is the probability that they will be associated in a fresh case in which one of them is known to be present;

(*b*) Under the same circumstances, a sufficient number of

cases of association will make the probability of a fresh association nearly a certainty, and will make it approach certainty without limit.

As just stated, the principle applies only to the verification of our expectation in a single fresh instance. But we want also to know that there is a probability in favour of the general law that things of the sort A are *always* associated with things of the sort B, provided a sufficient number of cases of association are known, and no cases of failure of association are known. The probability of the general law is obviously less than the probability of the particular case, since if the general law is true, the particular case must also be true, whereas the particular case may be true without the general law being true. Nevertheless the probability of the general law is increased by repetitions, just as the probability of the particular case is. We may therefore repeat the two parts of our principle as regards the general law, thus:

(*a*) The greater the number of cases in which a thing of the sort A has been found associated with a thing of the sort B, the more probable it is (if no cases of failure of association are known) that A is always associated with B;

(*b*) Under the same circumstances, a sufficient number of cases of the association of A with B will make it nearly certain that A is always associated with B, and will make this general law approach certainty without limit.

It should be noted that probability is always relative to certain data. In our case, the data are merely the known cases of coexistence of A and B. There may be other data, which *might* be taken into account, which would gravely alter the probability. For example, a man who had seen a great many white swans might argue, by our principle, that on the data it was *probable* that all swans were white, and this might be a perfectly sound argument. The argument is not disproved by the fact that some swans are black, because a thing may very well happen in spite of the fact that some data render it improbable. In the case of the swans, a man might know that colour is a very variable characteristic in many species of animals, and that, therefore, an induction as to colour is peculiarly liable to error. But this knowledge would be a fresh datum, by no means proving that the probability relatively to our previous data had been wrongly estimated. The fact, therefore, that things often fail to fulfil our expectations is no evidence that our expectations will not *probably* be fulfilled in a given case or a given class of cases. Thus our inductive principle is at any rate not capable of being *disproved* by an appeal to experience.

The inductive principle, however, is equally incapable of being *proved* by an appeal to experience. Experience might conceivably confirm the inductive principle as regards the cases that have been already examined; but as regards unexamined cases, it is the inductive principle alone that can justify any inference from what has been examined to what has not been examined. All arguments which, on the basis of experience, argue as to the future or the unexperienced parts of the past or present, assume the inductive principle; hence we can never use experience to prove the inductive principle without begging the question. Thus we must either accept the inductive principle on the ground of its intrinsic evidence, or forgo all justification of our expectations about the future. If the principle is unsound, we have no reason to expect the sun to rise to-morrow, to expect bread to be more nourishing than a stone, or to expect that if we throw ourselves off the roof we shall fall. When we see what looks like our best friend approaching us, we shall have no reason to suppose that his body is not inhabited by the mind of our worst enemy or of some total stranger. All our conduct is based upon associations which have worked in the past, and which we therefore regard as likely to work in the future; and this likelihood is dependent for its validity upon the inductive principle.

The general principles of science, such as the belief in the reign of law, and the belief that every event must have a cause, are as completely dependent upon the inductive principle as are the beliefs of daily life. All such general principles are believed because mankind have found innumerable instances of their truth and no instances of their falsehood. But this affords no evidence for their truth in the future, unless the inductive principle is assumed.

Thus all knowledge which, on a basis of experience tells us something about what is not experienced, is based upon a belief which experience can neither confirm nor confute, yet which, at least in its more concrete applications, appears to be as firmly rooted in us as many of the facts of experience. The existence and justification of such beliefs—for the inductive principle, as we shall see, is not the only example—raises some of the most difficult and most debated problems of philosophy.

LOGIC AS THE
ESSENCE OF PHILOSOPHY[1]

The topics we discussed in our first lecture, and the topics we shall discuss later, all reduce themselves, in so far as they are genuinely philosophical, to problems of logic. This is not due to any accident, but to the fact that every philosophical problem, when it is subjected to the necessary analysis and purification, is found either to be not really philosophical at all, or else to be, in the sense in which we are using the word, logical. But as the word "logic" is never used in the same sense by two different philosophers, some explanation of what I mean by the word is indispensable at the outset.

Logic, in the Middle Ages, and down to the present day in

---

[1] Reprinted from Bertrand Russell, *Our Knowledge of the External World* (London: George Allen & Unwin Ltd, 1914). By permission.

teaching, meant no more than a scholastic collection of technical terms and rules of syllogistic inference. Aristotle had spoken, and it was the part of humbler men merely to repeat the lesson after him. The trivial nonsense embodied in this tradition is still set in examinations, and defended by eminent authorities as an excellent "propædeutic," i.e. a training in those habits of solemn humbug which are so great a help in later life. But it is not this that I mean to praise in saying that all philosophy is logic. Ever since the beginning of the seventeenth century, all vigorous minds that have concerned themselves with inference have abandoned the mediæval tradition, and in one way or other have widened the scope of logic.

The first extension was the introduction of the inductive method by Bacon and Galileo—by the former in a theoretical and largely mistaken form, by the latter in actual use in establishing the foundations of modern physics and astronomy. This is probably the only extension of the old logic which has become familiar to the general educated public. But induction, important as it is when regarded as a method of investigation, does not seem to remain when its work is done: in the final form of a perfected science, it would seem that everything ought to be deductive. If induction remains at all, which is a difficult question, it will remain merely as one of the principles according to which deductions are effected. Thus the ultimate result of the introduction of the inductive method seems not the creation of a new kind of non-deductive reasoning, but rather the widening of the scope of deduction by pointing out a way of deducing which is certainly not syllogistic, and does not fit into the mediæval scheme.

* * *

Hegel and his followers widened the scope of logic in quite a different way—a way which I believe to be fallacious, but which requires discussion if only to show how their conception of logic differs from the conception which I wish to advocate. In their writings, logic is practically identical with metaphysics. In broad outline, the way this came about is as follows. Hegel believed

that, by means of *a priori* reasoning, it could be shown that the
world *must* have various important and interesting characteristics, since any world without these characteristics would be
impossible and self-contradictory. Thus what he calls "logic" is
an investigation of the nature of the universe, in so far as this
can be inferred merely from the principle that the universe
must be logically self-consistent. I do not myself believe that
from this principle alone anything of importance can be inferred as regards the existing universe. But, however that may
be, I should not regard Hegel's reasoning, even if it were valid,
as properly belonging to logic: it would rather be an application of logic to the actual world. Logic itself would be concerned rather with such questions as what self-consistency is,
which Hegel, so far as I know, does not discuss. And though he
critcizes the traditional logic, and professes to replace it by an
improved logic of his own, there is some sense in which the
traditional logic, with all its faults, is uncritically and unconsciously assumed throughout his reasoning. It is not in the direction advocated by him, it seems to me, that the reform of
logic is to be sought, but by a more fundamental, more patient,
and less ambitious investigation into the presuppositions which
his system shares with those of most other philosophers.

The way in which, as it seems to me, Hegel's system assumes
the ordinary logic which it subsequently criticizes, is exemplified by the general conception of "categories" with which he
operates throughout. This conception is, I think, essentially a
product of logical confusion, but it seems in some way to stand
for the conception of "qualities of Reality as a whole." Mr.
Bradley has worked out a theory according to which, in all judgment, we are ascribing a predicate to Reality as a whole; and
this theory is derived from Hegel. Now the traditional logic
holds that every proposition ascribes a predicate to a subject,
and from this it easily follows that there can be only one subject, the Absolute, for if there were two, the proposition that
there were two would not ascribe a predicate to either. Thus
Hegel's doctrine, that philosophical propositions must be of the
form, "the Absolute is such-and-such," depends upon the tra-

ditional belief in the universality of the subject-predicate form. This belief, being traditional, scarcely self-conscious, and not supposed to be important, operates underground, and is assumed in arguments which, like the refutation of relations, appear at first sight such as to establish its truth. This is the most important respect in which Hegel uncritically assumes the traditional logic. Other less important respects—though important enough to be the source of such essentially Hegelian con ceptions as the "concrete universal" and the "union of identity in difference"—will be found where he explicitly deals with formal logic.[2]

There is quite another direction in which a large technical development of logic has taken place: I mean the direction of what is called logistic or mathematical logic. This kind of logic is mathematical in two different senses: it is itself a branch of mathematics, and it is the logic which is specially applicable to other more traditional branches of mathematics. Historically, it began as *merely* a branch of mathematics: its special applicability to other branches is a more recent development. In both respects, it is the fulfilment of a hope which Leibniz cherished throughout his life, and pursued with all the ardour of his amazing intellectual energy. Much of his work on this subject has been published recently, since his discoveries have been remade by others; but none was published by him, because his results persisted in contradicting certain points in the traditional doctrine of the syllogism. We now know that on these points the traditional doctrine is wrong, but respect for Aristotle prevented Leibniz from realizing that this was possible.

The modern development of mathematical logic dates from Boole's *Laws of Thought* (1854). But in him and his successors, before Peano and Frege, the only thing really achieved, apart from certain details, was the invention of a mathematical sym-

---

[2] See the translation by H. S. Macran, *Hegel's Doctrine of Formal Logic*, Oxford, 1912. Hegel's argument in this portion of his "Logic" depends throughout upon confusing the "is" of predication, as in "Socrates is mortal," with the "is" of identity, as in "Socrates is the philosopher who drank the hemlock." Owing to this confusion, he thinks that "Socrates" and "mortal" must be identical. Seeing that they are different, he does not infer, as others would, that there is a mistake somewhere, but that they exhibit "identity in difference. . . ."

bolism for deducing consequences from the premises which the
newer methods shared with those of Aristotle. This subject has
considerable interest as an independent branch of mathematics,
but it has very little to do with real logic. The first serious advance in real logic since the time of the Greeks was made independently by Peano and Frege—both mathematicians. They
both arrived at their logical results by an analysis of mathematics. Traditional logic regarded the two propositions, "Socrates is mortal" and "All men are mortal," as being of the same
form;[3] Peano and Frege showed that they are utterly different
in form. The philosophical importance of logic may be illus-
trated by the fact that this confusion—which is still committed
by most writers—obscured not only the whole study of the
forms of judgment and inference, but also the relations of
things to their qualities, of concrete existence to abstract concepts, and of the world of sense to the world of Platonic ideas.
Peano and Frege, who pointed out the error, did so for technical reasons, and applied their logic mainly to technical developments; but the philosophical importance of the advance
which they made is impossible to exaggerate.

Mathematical logic, even in its most modern form, is not
directly of philosophical importance except in its beginnings.
After the beginnings, it belongs rather to mathematics than to
philosophy. Of its beginnings, which are the only part of it that
can properly be called *philosophical* logic, I shall speak shortly.
But even the later developments, though not directly philosophical, will be found of great indirect use in philosophizing.
They enable us to deal easily with more abstract conceptions
than merely verbal reasoning can enumerate; they suggest fruitful hypotheses which otherwise could hardly be thought of; and
they enable us to see quickly what is the smallest store of materials with which a given logical or scientific edifice can be
constructed. Not only Frege's theory of number, which we shall
deal with in Lecture VII, but the whole theory of physical con-

---

[3] It was often recognized that there was *some* difference between them, but it
was not recognized that the difference is fundamental, and of very great importance.

cepts which will be outlined in our next two lectures, is inspired by mathematical logic, and could never have been imagined without it.

In both these cases, and in many others, we shall appeal to a certain principle called "the principle of abstraction." This principle, which might equally well be called "the principle which dispenses with abstraction," and is one which clears away incredible accumulations of metaphysical lumber, was directly suggested by mathematical logic, and could hardly have been proved or practically used without its help. The principle will be explained in our fourth lecture, but its use may be briefly indicated in advance. When a group of objects have that kind of similarity which we are inclined to attribute to possession of a common quality, the principle in question shows that membership of the group will serve all the purposes of the supposed common quality, and that therefore, unless some common quality is actually known, the group or class of similar objects may be used to replace the common quality, which need not be assumed to exist. In this and other ways, the indirect uses of even the later parts of mathematical logic are very great; but it is now time to turn our attention to its philosophical foundations.

In every proposition and in every inference there is, besides the particular subject-matter concerned, a certain *form*, a way in which the constituents of the proposition or inference are put together. If I say, "Socrates is mortal," "Jones is angry," "The sun is hot," there is something in common in these three cases, something indicated by the word "is." What is in common is the *form* of the proposition, not an actual constituent. If I say a number of things about Socrates—that he was an Athenian, that he married Xantippe, that he drank the hemlock—there is a common constituent, namely Socrates, in all the propositions I enunciate, but they have diverse forms. If, on the other hand, I take any one of these propositions and replace its constituents, one at a time, by other constituents, the form remains constant, but no constituent remains. Take (say) the series of propositions, "Socrates drank the hemlock," "Coleridge drank the hemlock," "Coleridge drank opium," "Coleridge ate opium." The form remains unchanged throughout this series, but all the constituents are altered. Thus form is not another constituent, but is the way the constituents are put together. It is forms, in this sense, that are the proper object of philosophical logic.

It is obvious that the knowledge of logical forms is something quite different from knowledge of existing things. The form of "Socrates drank the hemlock" is not an existing thing like Socrates or the hemlock, nor does it even have that close relation to existing things that drinking has. It is something altogether more abstract and remote. We might understand all the separate words of a sentence without understanding the sentence: if a sentence is long and complicated, this is apt to happen. In such a case we have knowledge of the constituents, but not of the form. We may also have knowledge of the form without having knowledge of the constituents. If I say, "Rorarius drank the hemlock," those among you who have never heard of Rorarius (supposing there are any) will understand the form, without having knowledge of all the constituents. In order to understand a sentence, it is necessary to have knowledge both of the constituents and of the particular instance of the form. It is in this way that a sentence conveys information, since it tells us that certain known objects are related according to a certain known form. Thus some kind of knowledge of logical forms, though with most people it is not explicit, is involved in all understanding of discourse. It is the business of philosophical logic to extract this knowledge from its concrete integuments, and to render it explicit and pure.

In all inference, form alone is essential: the particular subject-matter is irrelevant except as securing the truth of the premisses. This is one reason for the great importance of logical form. When I say, "Socrates was a man, all men are mortal, therefore Socrates was mortal," the connection of premises and conclusion does not in any way depend upon its being Socrates and man and mortality that I am mentioning. The general form of the inference may be expressed in some such words as: "If a thing has a certain property, and whatever has this property has a certain other property, then the thing in question also has that other property." Here no particular things or properties are mentioned: the proposition is absolutely general. All inferences, when stated fully, are instances of propositions having this kind of generality. If they seem to depend upon the subject-matter otherwise than as regards the truth of the premises, that is because the premisses have not been all explicitly stated. In logic, it is a waste of time to deal with inferences concerning particular cases: we deal throughout with completely general and purely formal implications, leaving it to other sciences to discover when the hypotheses are verified and when they are not.

But the forms of propositions giving rise to inferences are not the simplest forms; they are always hypothetical, stating that if one proposition is true, then so is another. Before considering inference, therefore, logic must consider those simpler forms which inference presupposes. Here the traditional logic failed completely: it believed that there was only one form of simple proposition (i.e. of proposition not stating a relation between two or more other propositions), namely, the form which ascribes a predicate to a subject. This is the appropriate form in assigning the qualities of a given thing—we may say "this thing is round, and red, and so on." Grammar favours this form, but philosophically it is so far from universal that it is not even very common. If we say "this thing is bigger than that," we are not assigning a mere quality of "this," but a relation of "this" and "that." We might express the same fact by saying "that thing is smaller than this," where grammatically the subject is changed. Thus propositions stating that two things have a certain relation have a different form from subject-predicate propositions, and the failure to perceive this difference or to allow for it has been the source of many errors in traditional metaphysics.

The belief or unconscious conviction that all propositions are of the subject-predicate form—in other words: that every fact consists in some thing having some quality—has rendered most philosophers incapable of giving any account of the world of science and daily life. If they had been honestly anxious to

give such an account, they would probably have discovered
their error very quickly; but most of them were less anxious
to understand the world of science and daily life, than to con-
vict it of unreality in the interests of a super-sensible "real"
world. Belief in the unreality of the world of sense arises with
irresistible force in certain moods—moods which, I imagine,
have some simple physiological basis, but are none the less pow-
erfully persuasive. The conviction born of these moods is the
source of most mysticism and of most metaphysics. When the
emotional intensity of such a mood subsides, a man who is in
the habit of reasoning will search for logical reasons in favour
of the belief which he finds in himself. But since the belief
already exists, he will be very hospitable to any reason that
suggests itself. The paradoxes apparently proved by his logic
are really the paradoxes of mysticism, and are the goal which
he feels his logic must reach if it is to be in accordance with
insight. It is in this way that logic has been pursued by those
of the great philosophers who were mystics—notably Plato,
Spinoza, and Hegel. But since they usually took for granted the
supposed insight of the mystic emotion, their logical doctrines
were presented with a certain dryness, and were believed by
their disciples to be quite independent of the sudden illumina-
tion from which they sprang. Nevertheless their origin clung
to them, and they remained—to borrow a useful word from
Mr. Santayana—"malicious" in regard to the world of science
and common sense. It is only so that we can account for the
complacency with which philosophers have accepted the incon-
sistence of their doctrines with all the common and scientific
facts which seem best established and most worthy of belief.

The logic of mysticism shows, as is natural, the defects which
are inherent in anything malicious. While the mystic mood is
dominant, the need of logic is not felt; as the mood fades, the
impulse to logic reasserts itself, but with a desire to retain the
vanishing insight, or at least to prove that it *was* insight, and
that what seems to contradict it is illusion. The logic which
thus arises is not quite disinterested or candid, and is inspired
by a certain hatred of the daily world to which it is to be ap-

plied. Such an attitude naturally does not tend to the best results. Everyone knows that to read an author simply in order
to refute him is not the way to understand him; and to read the
book of Nature with a conviction that it is all illusion is just as
unlikely to lead to understanding. If our logic is to find the
common world intelligible, it must not be hostile, but must be
inspired by a genuine acceptance such as is not usually to be
found among metaphysicians.

Traditional logic, since it holds that all propositions have the
subject-predicate form, is unable to admit the reality of relations: all relations, it maintains, must be reduced to properties
of the apparently related terms. There are many ways of refut-
ing this opinion; one of the easiest is derived from the consideration of what are called "asymmetrical" relations. In order
to explain this, I will first explain two independent ways of
classifying relations.

Some relations, when they hold between A and B, also hold
between B and A. Such, for example, is the relation "brother
or sister." If A is a brother or sister of B then B is a brother or
sister of A. Such again is any kind of similarity, say similarity
of colour. Any kind of dissimilarity is also of this kind: if the
colour of A is unlike the colour of B, then the colour of B is
unlike the colour of A. Relations of this sort are called *symmetrical*. Thus a relation is symmetrical if, whenever it holds
between A and B, it also holds between B and A.

All relations that are not symmetrical are called *non-symmetrical*. Thus "brother" is non-symmetrical, because, if A is a
brother of B, it may happen that B is a *sister* of A.

A relation is called *asymmetrical* when, if it holds between
A and B, it *never* holds between B and A. Thus husband, father,
grandfather, etc., are asymmetrical relations. So are *before, after,
greater, above, to the right of,* etc. All the relations that give rise
to series are of this kind.

Classification into symmetrical, asymmetrical and merely non-
symmetrical relations is the first of the two classifications we
had to consider. The second is into transitive, intransitive, and
merely non-transitive relations, which are defined as follows.

A relation is said to be *transitive,* if, whenever it holds between A and B and also between B and C, it holds between A and C. Thus *before, after, greater, above* are transitive. All relations giving rise to series are transitive, but so are many others. The transitive relations just mentioned were asymmetrical, but many transitive relations are symmetrical—for instance, equality in any respect, exact identity of colour, being equally numerous (as applied to collections), and so on.

A relation is said to be *non-transitive* whenever it is not transitive. Thus "brother" is non-transitive, because a brother of one's brother may be oneself. All kinds of dissimilarity are non-transitive.

A relation is said to be *intransitive* when, if A has the relation to B, and B to C, A never has it to C. Thus "father" is intransitive. So is such a relation as "one inch taller" or "one year later."

Let us now, in the light of this classification, return to the question whether all relations can be reduced to predications.

In the case of symmetrical relations—i.e. relations which, if they hold between A and B, also hold between B and A—some kind of plausibility can be given to this doctrine. A symmetrical relation which is transitive, such as equality, can be regarded as expressing possession of some common property, while one which is not transitive, such as inequality, can be regarded as expressing possession of different properties. But when we come to asymmetrical relations, such as before and after, greater and less, etc., the attempt to reduce them to properties becomes obviously impossible. When, for example, two things are merely known to be unequal, without our knowing which is greater, we may say that the inequality results from their having different magnitudes, because inequality is a symmetrical relation; but to say that when one thing is *greater* than another, and not merely unequal to it, that means that they have different magnitudes, is formally incapable of explaining the facts. For if the other thing had been greater than the one, the magnitudes would also have been different, though the fact to be explained would not have been the same. Thus mere *difference* of magnitude is not *all* that is involved, since, if it were, there would be no difference between one thing being greater than another, and the other being greater than the one. We shall have to say that the one magnitude is *greater* than the *other*, and thus we shall have failed to get rid of the relation "greater." In short, both possession of the same property and possession of different properties are *symmetrical* relations, and therefore cannot account for the existence of *asymmetrical* relations.

Asymmetrical relations are involved in all series—in space and time, greater and less, whole and part, and many others of the most important characteristics of the actual world. All these aspects, therefore, the logic which reduces everything to subjects and predicates is compelled to condemn as error and mere appearance. To those whose logic is not malicious, such a wholesale condemnation appears impossible. And in fact there is no reason except prejudice, so far as I can discover, for denying the reality of relations. When once their reality is admitted, all *logical* grounds for supposing the world of sense to be illusory disappear. If this is to be supposed, it must be frankly and simply on the ground of mystic insight unsupported by argument. It is impossible to argue against what professes to be insight, so long as it does not argue in its own favour. As logicians, therefore, we may admit the possibility of the mystic's world, while yet, so long as we do not have his insight, we must continue to study the everyday world with which we are familiar. But when he contends that our world is impossible, then our logic is ready to repel his attack. And the first step in creating the logic which is to perform this service is the recognition of the reality of relations.

Relations which have two terms are only one kind of relations. A relation may have three terms, or four, or any number. Relations of two terms, being the simplest, have received more attention than the others, and have generally been alone considered by philosophers, both those who accepted and those who denied the reality of relations. But other relations have their importance, and are indispensable in the solution of certain problems. Jealousy, for example, is a relation between three people. Professor Royce mentions the relation "giving": when A gives B to C, that is a relation of three terms. When a man says to his wife: "My dear, I wish you could induce Angelina to accept Edwin," his wish constitutes a relation between four people, himself, his wife, Angelina, and Edwin. Thus such relations are by no means recondite or rare. But in order to explain exactly how they differ from relations of two terms, we must embark upon a classification of the logical forms of facts, which is the first business of logic, and the business in which the traditional logic has been most deficient.

The existing world consists of many things with many qualities and relations. A complete description of the existing world would require not only a catalogue of the things, but also a mention of all their qualities and relations. We should have to know not only this that, and the other thing, but also which was red, which yellow, which was earlier than which, which was which between two others, and so on. When I speak of a "fact," I do not mean one of the simple things in the world; I mean that a certain thing has a certain quality, or that certain things have a certain relation. Thus, for example, I should not call Napoleon a fact, but I should call it a fact that he was ambitious, or that he married Josephine. Now a fact, in this sense, is never simple, but always has two or more constituents. When it simply assigns a quality to a thing, it has only two constituents, the thing and the quality. When it consists of a relation between two things, it has three constituents, the things and the relation. When it consists of a relation between three things, it has four constituents, and so on. The constituents of facts, in the sense in which we are using the word "fact," are not other facts, but are things and qualities or relations. When we say that there are relations of more than two terms, we mean that there are single facts consisting of a single relation and more than two things. I do not mean that one relation of two terms may hold between A and B, and also between A and C, as, for example, a man is the son of his father and also the son of his mother. This constitutes two distinct facts: if we choose to treat it as one fact, it is a fact which has facts for its constituents. But the facts I am speaking of have no facts among their constituents, but only things and relations. For example, when A is jealous of B on account of C, there is only one fact, involving three people; there are not two instances of jealousy, but only one. It is in such cases that I speak of a relation of three terms, where the simplest possible fact in which the relation occurs is one involving three things in addition to the relation. And the same applies to relations of four terms or five or any other number. All such relations must be admitted in our inventory of the logical forms of facts: two facts involving the same number of things have the same form, and two which involve different numbers of things have different forms.

Given any fact, there is an assertion which expresses the fact. The fact itself is objective, and independent of our thought or opinion about it; but the assertion is something which involves thought, and may be either true or false. An assertion may be positive or negative: we may assert that Charles I was executed, or that he did *not* die in his bed. A negative assertion may be said to be a *denial*. Given a form of words which must be either true or false, such as "Charles I died in his bed," we may either assert or deny this form of words: in the one case we have a positive assertion, in the other a negative one. A form of words which must be either true or false I shall call a *proposition*. Thus a proposition is the same as what may be significantly asserted or denied. A proposition which expresses what we have called a fact, i.e. which, when asserted, asserts that a certain thing has a certain quality, or that certain things have a certain relation, will be called an atomic proposition, because, as we shall see immediately, there are other propositions into which atomic propositions enter in a way analogous to that in which atoms enter into molecules. Atomic propositions, although, like facts, they may have any one of an infinite number of forms, are only one kind of propositions. All other kinds are more complicated. In order to preserve the parallelism in language as regards facts and propositions, we shall give the name "atomic facts" to the facts we have hitherto been considering. Thus atomic facts are what determine whether atomic propositions are to be asserted or denied.

Whether an atomic proposition, such as "this is red," or "this is before that," is to be asserted or denied can only be known empirically. Perhaps one atomic fact may sometimes be capable of being inferred from another, though this seems very doubtful; but in any case it cannot be inferred from premisses no one of which is an atomic fact. It follows that, if atomic facts are to be known at all, some at least must be known without inference. The atomic facts which we come to know in this way are the facts of sense-perception; at any rate, the facts of sense-perception are those which we most obviously and certainly come to know in this way. If we knew all atomic facts, and also knew that there were none except those we knew, we should, theoretically, be able to infer all truths of whatever form.[4] Thus logic would then supply us with the whole of the apparatus required. But in the first acquisition of knowledge concerning atomic facts, logic is useless. In pure logic, no atomic fact is ever mentioned: we confine ourselves wholly to forms, without asking ourselves what objects can fill the forms. Thus pure logic is independent of atomic facts; but conversely, they are, in a sense, independent of logic. Pure logic and atomic facts are the two poles, the wholly *a priori* and the wholly empirical. But between the two lies a vast intermediate region, which we must now briefly explore.

"Molecular" propositions are such as contain conjunctions— *if, or, and, unless,* etc.—and such words are the marks of a molecular proposition. Consider such an assertion as, "If it rains, I shall bring my umbrella." This assertion is just as capable of truth or falsehood as the assertion of an atomic proposition, but it is obvious that either the corresponding fact, or the nature of the correspondence with fact, must be quite different from what it is in the case of an atomic proposition. Whether it rains, and whether I bring my umbrella, are each severally matters of

---

[4] This perhaps requires modification in order to include such facts as beliefs and wishes, since such facts apparently contain propositions as components. Such facts, though not strictly atomic, must be supposed included if the statement in the text is to be true.

atomic fact, ascertainable by observation. But the connection of the two involved in saying that *if* the one happens, *then* the other will happen, is something radically different from either of the two separately. It does not require for its truth that it should actually rain, or that I should actually bring my umbrella; even if the weather is cloudless, it may still be true that I should have brought my umbrella if the weather had been different. Thus we have here a connection of two propositions, which does not depend upon whether they are to be asserted or denied, but only upon the second being inferable from the first. Such propositions, therefore, have a form which is different from that of any atomic proposition.

Such propositions are important to logic, because all inference depends upon them. If I have told you that if it rains I shall bring my umbrella, and if you see that there is a steady downpour, you can infer that I shall bring my umbrella. There can be no inference except where propositions are connected in some such way, so that from the truth or falsehood of the one something follows as to the truth or falsehood of the other. It seems to be the case that we can sometimes know molecular propositions, as in the above instance of the umbrella, when we do not know whether the component atomic propositions are true or false. The *practical* utility of inference rests upon this fact.

The next kind of propositions we have to consider are *general* propositions, such as "all men are mortal," "all equilateral triangles are equiangular." And with these belong propositions in which the word "some" occurs, such as "some men are philosophers" or "some philosophers are not wise." These are the denials of general propositions, namely (in the above instances), of "all men are non-philosophers" and "all philosophers are wise." We will call propositions containing the word "some" *negative* general propositions, and those containing the word "all" *positive* general propositions. These propositions, it will be seen, begin to have the appearance of the propositions in logical text-books. But their peculiarity and complexity are not known to the text-books, and the problems which they raise are only discussed in the most superficial manner.

When we were discussing atomic facts, we saw that we should be able, theoretically, to infer all other truths by logic if we knew all atomic facts and also knew that there were no other atomic facts besides those we knew. The knowledge that there are no other atomic facts is positive general knowledge; it is the knowledge that "all atomic facts are known to me," or at least "all atomic facts are in this collection"—however the collection may be given. It is easy to see that general propositions, such as "all men are mortal," cannot be known by inference from atomic facts alone. If we could know each individual man, and know that he was mortal, that would not enable us to know that all men are mortal, unless we *knew* that those were all the men there are, which is a general proposition. If we knew every other existing thing throughout the universe, and knew that each separate thing was not an immortal man, that would not give us our result unless we *knew* that we had explored the whole universe, i.e. unless we knew "all things belong to this collection of things I have examined." Thus general truths cannot be inferred from particular truths alone, but must, if they are to be known, be either self-evident or inferred from premisses of which at least one is a general truth. But all *empirical* evidence is of *particular* truths. Hence, if there is any knowledge of general truths at all, there must be *some* knowledge of general truths which is independent of empirical evidence, i.e. does not depend upon the data of sense.

The above conclusion, of which we had an instance in the case of the inductive principle, is important, since it affords a refutation of the older empiricists. They believed that all our knowledge is derived from the senses and dependent upon them. We see that, if this view is to be maintained, we must refuse to admit that we know any general propositions. It is perfectly possible logically that this should be the case, but it does not appear to be so in fact, and indeed no one would dream of maintaining such a view except a theorist at the last extremity. We must therefore admit that there is general knowledge not derived from sense, and that some of this knowledge is not obtained by inference but is primitive.

Such general knowledge is to be found in logic. Whether there is any such knowledge not derived from logic, I do not know; but in logic, at any rate, we have such knowledge. It will be remembered that we excluded from pure logic such propositions as, "Socrates is a man, all men are mortal, therefore Socrates is mortal," because Socrates and *man* and *mortal* are empirical terms, only to be understood through particular experience. The corresponding proposition in pure logic is: "If anything has a certain property, and whatever has this property has a certain other property, then the thing in question has the other property." This proposition is absolutely general: it applies to all things and all properties. And it is quite self-evident. Thus in such propositions of pure logic we have the self-evident general propositions of which we were in search.

A proposition such as "If Socrates is a man, and all men are mortal, then Socrates is mortal," is true in virtue of its *form* alone. Its truth, in this hypothetical form, does not depend upon whether Socrates actually is a man, nor upon whether in fact all men are mortal; thus it is equally true when we substitute other terms for Socrates and *man* and *mortal*. The general truth of which it is an instance is purely formal, and belongs to logic. Since this general truth does not mention any particular thing, or even any particular quality or relation, it is wholly independent of the accidental facts of the existent world, and can be known, theoretically, without any experience of particular things or their qualities and relations.

Logic, we may say, consists of two parts. The first part investigates what propositions are and what forms they may have; this part enumerates the different kinds of atomic propositions, of molecular propositions, of general propositions, and so on. The second part consists of certain supremely general propositions, which assert the truth of all propositions of certain forms. This second part merges into pure mathematics, whose propositions all turn out, on analysis, to be such general formal truths. The first part, which merely enumerates forms, is the more difficult, and philosophically the more important; and it is the recent progress in this first part, more than anything else, that has rendered a truly scientific discussion of many philosophical problems possible.

The problem of the nature of judgment or belief may be taken as an example of a problem whose solution depends upon an adequate inventory of logical forms. We have already seen how the supposed universality of the subject-predicate form made it impossible to give a right analysis of serial order, and therefore made space and time unintelligible. But in this case it was only necessary to admit relations of two terms. The case of judgment demands the admission of more complicated forms. If all judgments were true, we might suppose that a judgment consisted in apprehension of a *fact,* and that the apprehension was a relation of a mind to the fact. From poverty in the logical inventory, this view has often been held. But it leads to absolutely insoluble difficulties in the case of error. Suppose I believe that Charles I died in his bed. There is no objective fact "Charles I's death in his bed" to which I can have a relation of apprehension. Charles I and death and his bed are objective, but they are not, except in my thought, put together as my false belief supposes. It is therefore necessary, in analysing a belief, to look for some other logical form than a two-term relation. Failure to realize this necessity has, in my opinion, vitiated almost everything that has hitherto been written on the theory of knowledge, making the problem of error insoluble and the difference between belief and perception inexplicable.

Modern logic, as I hope is now evident, has the effect of enlarging our abstract imagination, and providing an infinite number of possible hypotheses to be applied in the analysis of any complex fact. In this respect it is the exact opposite of the logic practised by the classical tradition. In that logic, hypotheses which seem *prima facie* possible are professedly proved impossible, and it is decreed in advance that reality must have a certain special character. In modern logic, on the contrary, while the *prima facie* hypotheses as a rule remain admissible, others, which only logic would have suggested, are added to our stock, and are very often found to be indispensable if a right analysis of the facts is to be obtained. The old logic put thought in fetters, while the new logic gives it wings. It has, in my opinion, introduced the same kind of advance into philosophy as Galileo introduced into physics, making it possible at last to see what kinds of problems may be capable of solution, and what kinds must be abandoned as beyond human powers. And where a solution appears possible, the new logic provides a method which enables us to obtain results that do not merely embody personal idiosyncracies, but must command the assent of all who are competent to form an opinion.

ARISTOTLE'S LOGIC[1]

Aristotle's influence, which was very great in many different fields, was greatest of all in logic. In late antiquity, when Plato was still supreme in metaphysics, Aristotle was the recognized authority in logic, and he retained this position throughout the Middle Ages. It was not till the thirteenth century that Christian philosophers accorded him supremacy in the field of metaphysics. This supremacy was largely lost after the Renaissance, but his supremacy in logic survived. Even at the present day, all Catholic teachers of philosophy and many others still obstinately reject the discoveries of modern logic, and adhere with a strange tenacity to a system which is as definitely antiquated as Ptolemaic astronomy. This makes it difficult to do historical justice to Aristotle. His present-day influence is so inimical to clear thinking that it is hard to remember how great an advance he made upon all his predecessors (including Plato), or how admirable his logical work would still seem if it had been a stage in a continual progress, instead of being (as in fact it was) a dead end, followed by over two thousand years

---

[1] From *A History of Western Philosophy*, copyright, 1945, by Bertrand Russell. Reprinted by permission of Simon and Schuster, Inc.

of stagnation. In dealing with the predecessors of Aristotle, it is not necessary to remind the reader that they are not verbally inspired; one can therefore praise them for their ability without being supposed to subscribe to all their doctrines. Aristotle, on the contrary, is still, especially in logic, a battle-ground, and cannot be treated in a purely historical spirit.

Aristotle's most important work in logic is the doctrine of the syllogism. A syllogism is an argument consisting of three parts, a major premiss, a minor premiss, and a conclusion. Syllogisms are of a number of different kinds, each of which has a name given by the scholastics. The most familiar is the kind called 'Barbara':

> All men are mortal (Major premiss).
> Socrates is a man (Minor premiss).
> Therefore: Socrates is mortal (Conclusion).
>
> Or: all men are mortal.
> All Greeks are men.
> Therefore: All Greeks are mortal.

(Aristotle does not distinguish between these two forms; this, as we shall see later, is a mistake.)

Other forms are: No fishes are rational, all sharks are fishes, therefore no sharks are rational. (This is called 'Celarent.')

All men are rational, some animals are men, therefore some animals are rational. (This is called 'Darii.')

No Greeks are black, some men are Greeks, therefore some men are not black. (This is called 'Ferio.')

These four make up the 'first figure'; Aristotle adds a second and third figure, and the schoolmen added a fourth. It is shown that the three later figures can be reduced to the first by various devices.

There are some inferences that can be made from a single premiss. From 'some men are mortal' we can infer that 'some mortals are men.' According to Aristotle, this can be also inferred from 'all men are mortal.' From 'no gods are mortal' we can infer 'no mortals are gods,' but from 'some men are not Greeks' it does not follow that 'some Greeks are not men.'

Apart from such inferences as the above, Aristotle and his followers thought that all deductive inference, when strictly stated, is syllogistic. By setting forth all the valid kinds of syllogism, and setting out any suggested argument in syllogistic form, it should therefore be possible to avoid all fallacies.

This system was the beginning of formal logic, and, as such, was both important and admirable. But considered as the end, not the beginning, of formal logic, it is open to three kinds of criticism:

(1) Formal defects within the system itself.
(2) Over-estimation of the syllogism, as compared to other forms of deductive argument.
(3) Over-estimation of deduction as a form of argument.

On each of these three, something must be said.

(1) *Formal defects.* Let us begin with the two statements 'Socrates is a man' and 'all Greeks are men.' It is necessary to make a sharp distinction between these two, which is not done in Aristotelian logic. The statement 'all Greeks are men' is commonly interpreted as implying that there are Greeks; without this implication, some of Aristotle's syllogisms are not valid. Take for instance:

'All Greeks are men, all Greeks are white, therefore some men are white.' This is valid if there are Greeks, but not otherwise. If I were to say:

'All golden mountains are mountains, all golden mountains are golden, therefore some mountains are golden,' my conclusion would be false, though in some sense my premises would be true. If we are to be explicit, we must therefore divide the one statement 'all Greeks are men' into two, one saying 'there are Greeks,' and the other saying 'if anything is a Greek it is a man.' The latter statement is purely hypothetical, and does not imply that there are Greeks.

The statement 'all Greeks are men' is thus much more complex in form than the statement 'Socrates is a man.' 'Socrates is a man' has Socrates for its subject, but 'all Greeks are men' does not have 'all Greeks' for its subject, for there is nothing about 'all Greeks' either in the statement 'there are Greeks,' or in the statement 'if anything is a Greek it is a man.'

This purely formal error was a source of errors in metaphysics and theory of knowledge. Consider the state of our knowledge in regard to the two propositions 'Socrates is mortal' and 'all men are mortal.' In order to know the truth of 'Socrates is mortal,' most of us are content to rely upon testimony; but if testimony is to be reliable, it must lead us back to some one who knew Socrates and saw him dead. The one perceived fact—the dead body of Socrates—together with the knowledge that this was called 'Socrates,' was enough to assure us of the mortality of Socrates. But when it comes to 'all men are mortal,' the matter is different. The question of our knowledge of such general propositions is a very difficult one. Sometimes they are merely verbal: 'all Greeks are men' is known because nothing is called 'a Greek' unless it is a man. Such general statements can be ascertained from the dictionary; they tell us nothing about the world except how words are used. But 'all men are mortal' is not of this sort; there is nothing logically self-contradictory about an immortal man. We believe the proposition on the basis of induction, because there is no well-authenticated case of a man living more than (say) one hundred and fifty years; but this only makes the proposition probable, not certain. It cannot be certain so long as living men exist.

Metaphysical errors arose through supposing that 'all men' is the subject of 'all men are mortal' in the same sense as that in which 'Socrates' is the subject of 'Socrates is mortal.' It made it possible to hold that, in some sense, 'all men' denotes an entity of the same sort as that denoted by 'Socrates.' This led Aristotle to say that in a sense a species is a substance. He is careful to qualify this statement, but his followers, especially Porphyry, showed less caution.

Another error into which Aristotle falls through this mistake is to think that a predicate of a predicate can be a predicate of the original subject. If I say 'Socrates is Greek, all Greeks are human,' Aristotle thinks that 'human' is a predicate of 'Greek,' while 'Greek' is a predicate of 'Socrates,' and obviously 'human' is a predicate of 'Socrates.' But in fact 'human' is not a predicate of 'Greek.' The distinction between names and predicates, or in metaphysical language, between particulars and universals, is thus blurred, with disastrous consequences to philosophy. One of the resulting confusions was to suppose that a class with only one member is identical with that one member. This made it impossible to have a correct theory of the number *one,* and led to endless bad metaphysics about unity.

(2) *Over-estimation of the syllogism.* The syllogism is only one kind of deductive argument. In mathematics, which is wholly deductive, syllogisms hardly ever occur. Of course, it would be possible to re-write mathematical arguments in syllogistic form, but this would be very artificial and would not make them any more cogent. Take arithmetic, for example. If I buy goods worth 16s. 3d., and tender a £1 note in payment, how much change is due to me? To put this simple sum in the form of a syllogism would be absurd, and would tend to conceal the real nature of the argument. Again, within logic there are non-syllogistic inferences such as: 'A horse is an animal, therefore a horse's head is an animal's head.' Valid syllogisms, in fact, are only some among valid deductions, and have no logical priority over others. The attempt to give pre-eminence to the syllogism in deduction misled philosophers as to the nature of mathematical reasoning. Kant, who perceived that mathematics is not syllogistic, inferred that it uses extra-logical principles, which, however, he supposed to be as certain as those of logic. He, like his predecessors, though in a different way, was misled by respect for Aristotle.

(3) *Over-estimation of deduction.* The Greeks in general attached more importance to deduction as a source of knowledge than modern philosophers do. In this respect, Aristotle was less at fault than Plato; he repeatedly admitted the importance of induction, and he devoted considerable attention to the question: how do we know the first premisses from which deduction must start? Nevertheless, he, like other Greeks, gave undue prominence to deduction in his theory of knowledge. We shall agree that Mr. Smith (say) is mortal, and we may, loosely, say

that we know that because we know that all men are mortal. But what we really know is not 'all men are mortal'; we know rather something like 'all men born more than one hundred and fifty years ago are mortal, and so are almost all men born more than one hundred years ago.' This is our reason for thinking that Mr. Smith will die. But this argument is an induction, not a deduction. It has less cogency than a deduction, and yields only a probability, not a certainty; but on the other hand it gives *new* knowledge, which deduction does not. All the important inferences outside logic and pure mathematics are inductive, not deductive; the only exceptions are law and theology, each of which derives its first principles from an unquestionable text, viz. the statute books or the scriptures.

Apart from *The Prior Analytics,* which deals with the syllogism, there are other logical writings of Aristotle which have considerable importance in the history of philosophy. One of these is the short work on *The Categories.* Porphyry the Neoplatonist wrote a commentary on this book, which had a very notable influence on medieval philosophy; but for the present let us ignore Porphyry and confine ourselves to Aristotle.

What, exactly, is meant by the word 'category,' whether in Aristotle or in Kant and Hegel, I must confess that I have never been able to understand. I do not myself believe that the term 'category' is in any way useful in philosophy, as representing any clear idea. There are, in Aristotle, ten categories: substance, quantity, quality, relation, place, time, position, state, action, and affection. The only definition offered of the term 'category' is: 'expressions which are in no way composite signify'—and then follows the above list. This seems to mean that every word of which the meaning is not compounded of the meanings of other words signifies a substance or a quantity or etc. There is no suggestion of any principle on which the list of ten categories has been compiled.

'Substance' is primarily what is not predicable of a subject nor present in a subject. A thing is said to be 'present in a subject' when, though not a part of the subject, it cannot exist without the subject. The instances given are a piece of grammatical knowledge which is present in a mind, and a certain whiteness which may be present in a body. A substance in the above primary sense is an individual thing or person or animal. But in a secondary sense a species or a genus—e.g. 'man' or 'animal'—may be called a substance. This secondary sense seems indefensible, and opened the door, in later writers, to much bad metaphysics.

The Posterior Analytics is a work largely concerned with a question which must trouble any deductive theory, namely: How are first premisses obtained? Since deduction must start from somewhere, we must begin with something unproved, which must be known otherwise than by demonstration. I shall not give Aristotle's theory in detail, since it depends upon the notion of *essence*. A definition, he says, is a statement of a thing's essential nature. The notion of essence is an intimate part of every philosophy subsequent to Aristotle, until we come to modern times. It is, in my opinion, a hopelessly muddleheaded notion, but its historical importance requires us to say something about it.

The 'essence' of a thing appears to have meant 'those of its properties which it cannot change without losing its identity.' Socrates may be sometimes happy, sometimes sad; sometimes well, sometimes ill. Since he can change these properties without ceasing to be Socrates, they are no part of his essence. But it is supposed to be of the essence of Socrates that he is a man, though a Pythagorean, who believes in transmigration, will not admit this. In fact, the question of 'essence' is one as to the use of words. We apply the same name, on different occasions, to somewhat different occurrences, which we regard as manifestations of a single 'thing' or 'person.' In fact, however, this is only a verbal convenience. The 'essence' of Socrates thus consists of those properties in the absence of which we should not use the name 'Socrates.' The question is purely linguistic: a *word* may have an essence, but a *thing* cannot.

The conception of 'substance,' like that of 'essence,' is a transference to metaphysics of what is only a linguistic convenience. We find it convenient, in describing the world, to describe a certain number of occurrences as events in the life of 'Socrates,' and a certain number of others as events in the life of 'Mr. Smith.' This leads us to think of 'Socrates' or 'Mr. Smith' as denoting something that persists through a certain number of years, and as in some way more 'solid' and 'real' than the events that happen to him. If Socrates is ill, we think that Socrates, at other times, is well, and therefore the being of Socrates is independent of his illness; illness, on the other hand, requires somebody to be ill. But although Socrates need not be ill, *something* must be occurring to him if he is to be considered to exist. He is not, therefore, really any more 'solid' than the things that happen to him.

'Substance,' when taken seriously, is a concept impossible to free from difficulties. A substance is supposed to be the subject of properties, and to be something distinct from all its properties. But when we take away the properties, and try to imagine the substance by itself, we find that there is nothing left. To put the matter in another way: What distinguishes one substance from another? Not difference of properties, for, according to the logic of substance, difference of properties presupposes numerical diversity between the substances concerned. Two substances, therefore, must be *just* two, without being, in themselves, in any way distinguishable. How, then, are we ever to find out that they *are* two?

'Substance,' in fact, is merely a convenient way of collecting events into bundles. What can we know about Mr. Smith? When we look at him, we see a pattern of colours; when we listen to him talking, we hear a series of sounds. We believe that, like us, he has thoughts and feelings. But what is Mr. Smith apart from all these occurrences? A mere imaginary hook, from which the occurrences are supposed to hang. They have in fact no need of a hook, any more than the earth needs an elephant to rest upon. Anyone can see, in the analogous case of a geographical region, that such a word as 'France' (say) is only a linguistic convenience, and that there is not a *thing* called 'France' over and above its various parts. The same holds of 'Mr. Smith'; it is a collective name for a number of occurrences. If we take it as anything more, it denotes something completely unknowable, and therefore not needed for the expression of what we know.

'Substance,' in a word, is a metaphysical mistake, due to transference to the world-structure of the structure of sentences composed of a subject and a predicate.

I conclude that the Aristotelian doctrines with which we have been concerned in this chapter are wholly false, with the exception of the formal theory of the syllogism, which is unimportant. Any person in the present day who wishes to learn logic will be wasting his time if he reads Aristotle or any of his disciples. None the less, Aristotle's logical writings show great ability, and would have been useful to mankind if they had appeared at a time when intellectual originality was still active. Unfortunately, they appeared at the very end of the creative period of Greek thought, and therefore came to be accepted as authoritative. By the time that logical originality revived, a reign of two thousand years had made Aristotle very difficult to dethrone. Throughout modern times, practically every advance in science, in logic, or in philosophy has had to be made in the teeth of opposition from Aristotle's disciples.

HENRY B. VEATCH

Distinguished Service Professor of Philosophy, Indiana University.

Given the present situation in logic (that is, the work of Russell and his followers), a student of traditional views can take one of several intersecting courses. He can extend the old logic and detach it from an unpopular metaphysics; he can reinterpret or refine the subtler and more complicated aspects of Aristotle's logic in terms of the aims and even the notation of the new logic; or he can try to forge from Aristotle a new defensive against the modern challenge. The first alternative is the more obvious;[1] the second alternative is the more difficult;[2] but the third may be the more heroic.[3]

Some heroes there have been—Johnson, Joseph, and Cook Wilson in England; and minor heroes there are in America—Maritain, Wick and Veatch. The last, however, stands in the Aristotelian tradition more loyally and polemically than any other. Nevertheless, though he sometimes speaks of Aristotelian logic, it is not an exposition of the master's views that Veatch intends, but a contemporary development of logical ideas which are planted within a framework of the Aristotelian, so-called "realistic," philosophy.

In the following essay only two aspects of the many-sided challenge of modern logic are considered, namely, the characterization of the subject matter itself and the logical character of propositions. Here, and throughout his logical writings, Veatch persistently presses the charge that the modern logician, willy-nilly, confuses two rather importantly different things: real relations in the world and logical relations in the proposition. Even if readers find something vaguely tendentious in this analysis, they will study the further theory with profit. Holding that the principal items of concern to the logician are concepts, propositions, and syllogisms,

---

[1] Quine, *Methods of Logic.*
[2] Lukasiewicz, *Aristotle's Syllogistic.*
[3] Veatch, *Intentional Logic.*

148

Veatch argues that each of these has a definite structure (here called "the relation of identity") and a definite instrumental function (here called "intentional"). Furthermore, the reality to which these conceptual instruments give us access is supposed to be that described by the Aristotelian metaphysics. It is a world of real causes, of substances and attributes, and of corresponding middle terms, categories, and predicables; logic does not remain philosophically uncommitted. Indeed, whereas Russell once held that the essence of philosophy is logic, Veatch holds, in effect, that the essence of logic is philosophy.

FORMALISM AND/OR
INTENTIONALITY IN LOGIC[1]

What is to be understood by the intentionality of Aristotelian logic? . . . Considering that realism involves among its basic tenets, (1) the principle that there are real things whose being or existence is independent of their being known, and (2) the principle that we human beings are at least partially capable of knowing these real beings as they are in themselves and not merely as they are relatively to us, then logic in such a realistic context becomes simply the instrument or organon of this human knowledge of the real.

Moreover, once logical entities are taken to be thus radically instrumental, they will perforce turn out to be radically intentional also. That is to say, their whole nature and being will consist simply in their meaning or signifying or "tending" toward the real which they are designed to disclose. In this sense the being of a concept is its being *of* something; and of a proposition, its being *about* something; and of an argument, its being

[1] Reprinted from Henry B. Veatch, *Philosophy and Phenomenological Research*, XI, No. 3 (March 1951). Some footnotes and several concluding paragraphs have been omitted.

in demonstration of something. Hence the study of logic and of logical entities will necessarily be the study of things whose very nature it is to mean or intend something other than themselves.

Further, as a direct consequence of this intentional character of logic, one can see how it would be quite impossible to study logical entities, so conceived, apart from their intentional reference. Indeed, one might even say that to study such logical entities is *eo ipso* to study how they are adapted to their function of intending or disclosing the real. Nor can one very well study such an adaptation to the business of revealing the being and nature of things, unless one also takes account of that very being and nature of things which these logical entities are thus adapted to disclose. It is in this sense, then, and precisely in this sense that we feel justified in declaring that any understanding of the intentionality of Aristotelian logic necessarily presupposes an understanding of the realism of Aristotelian metaphysics.

Now clearly, no such metaphysical setting characterizes modern mathematical logic. On the contrary, no modern logician would ever consider that the study of logic must involve any such metaphysical presupposition to the effect that in order to understand the nature and structure of the logical, one must first know something of the nature and structure of the real. In consequence, when the mathematical logician addresses himself to the task of investigating what he calls logical forms or structures or relations, he does not concern himself with whether and how such forms and structures differ from real forms and structures. Rather any formal structure, he would think, provided it be truly formal, in the sense of being abstracted from all content, would fall within the province of logic and/or mathematics.

Moreover, if such be the character of formalism in mathematical logic, we may note at once a number of salient points of difference between a logic so-conceived and an intentional logic of the Aristotelian type. For one thing, such a formal logic[2] can-

---

[2] By thus contrasting the intentionality of Aristotelian logic with the formalism of modern logic, we do not mean to imply that Aristotelian logic is nonformal. On the contrary, it is very much concerned with the forms of propositions, of syllogisms, and even, one might say, of concepts. And yet the point is,

not possibly be intentional in the Aristotelian sense, simply because it is not to be understood against that background of philosophical realism, which alone makes intentionality of the sort we have described intelligible. For another thing, whereas the mathematical logician would consider it his business to investigate any and all forms, provided only they be truly 'formal' and free from content, the Aristotelian logician would consider that, *qua* logician, he must confine his attention exclusively to the so-called intentional forms. In other words, the Aristotelian logician always presupposes that there is a distinction between properly logical (sc. intentional) forms and relations, and real forms and relations; and while he would not deny the importance of investigating such real relations and structures, he would insist that such is not the business of the logician, but rather of, say, the mathematician.

On the other hand, since in modern logic no distinction between so-called intentional forms and non-intentional forms is recognized, it follows that the very basis for any distinction between the logical and the real, in the Aristotelian sense, is obliterated. Not only that, but as we shall try to show in the course of our discussion, not only does the modern formalist in logic make no distinction between the logical and the real, but also, making no such distinction, he quite unconsciously treats of the properly logical forms and relations—propositions, arguments, etc.—as if they were real forms and relations, thereby eliminating all vestige of intentionality from them.

However, our theses are far outrunning our evidence. Hence, let us return for the present to a closer consideration of formalism in modern logic, to see if we can get a somewhat clearer notion of just what is meant by a logical form. Unfortunately, modern logicians are chary about declaring themselves too unequivocally on this score. But perhaps we might take a declaration of Bertrand Russell's as not being too unrepresentative.

"What are the constituents of a logical proposition?" [3] asks

that the forms which the Aristotelian logician concerns himself with he considers to be intentional forms exclusively, in contrast to all other non-intentional forms.

[3] By a "logical proposition," Russell here means, of course, a proposition in logic.

Russell. "I do not know the answer, but I propose to explain how the problem arises. Take (say) the proposition, 'Socrates was before Aristotle.' Here it seems obvious that we have a relation between two terms, and that the constituents of the proposition (as well as of the corresponding fact) are simply the two terms and the relation, i.e., Socrates, Aristotle, and *before*. . . . We may represent the general form of such propositions by 'x R y' which may be read 'x has the relation R to y.' This general form may occur in logical propositions, but no particular instance of it can occur. . . ."

Hence the conclusion that "no particular things or relations can ever enter a proposition of pure logic. We are left with pure *forms* as the only possible constituents of logical propositions." [4] In other words, logical propositions are propositions about pure forms, and the pure forms, to judge from Russell's example, turn out to be generalized relations.

Or as another illustration, we might consider an instance of what might be called a formal system in process of generation. Thus consider the case of two line segments that are congruent.[5] This situation might be simply described in the proposition:

"This segment is congruent to that."

Then, abstracting by successive stages, one gets:

"x is congruent to that segment."

"x is congruent to y."

"x R y."

Having reached, then, this pure form or abstract type of relation, designated by "R," one can actually determine its properties by constructing a whole formal system. Thus, as axioms, one might use:

Axiom I. For any element x of the class K,

   x R x.

Axiom II. For any elements, x, y, and z of K,

   if x R z and y R z, then x R y.

---

[4] *Introduction to Mathematical Philosophy* (second edition, London 1920), pp. 198-199.

[5] This example is based on Tarski, A., *Introduction to Logic* (second edition, New York, 1946), esp. p. 121.

From these would follow the various theorems, for example:
Theorem I. For any elements y and z of K, if y R z, then
z R y.
Theorem II. For any elements x, y and z of the class K,
if x R y and y R z, then x R z.

Here, clearly, we can see how "pure forms" of the type Russell had in mind emerge through a process of abstraction; and having thus emerged, they are then made to enter as constituents into what are wont to be called properly logical propositions—propositions, that is, containing no constants other than logical constants.[6] Moreover, once such logical propositions, treating as they do of these so-called pure forms, are enunciated, they can then be arranged in formal systems that are completely abstract and "uninterpreted." Such would be a truly formal logic in the modern sense.

Now from the Aristotelian point of view the interesting thing about these illustrations of what is meant by the purely formal subject matter of logic is that they do not involve properly logical forms at all. Thus the first example, drawn from Russell, concerned the relation of one man's being *before* another, and the other example involved one line segment's being *congruent* to another. But surely, there is nothing properly logical or intentional about a relation of temporal priority or a relation of spatial congruence. On the contrary, an Aristotelian would insist that these are *real* relations,[7] i.e., relations that might hold (and in the instances cited, relations that actually do hold) between individuals in the real world. Hence to consider that the in-

---

[6] Cf. Quine's characterization of a logical proposition as one in which only the logical elements occur *essentially,* all others *vacuously. Mathematical Logic* (Cambridge, 1947), pp. 1-2. . . .

[7] The term "real" in the expression "real relation" demands some explanation. In the first place, it should be noted that we take the real to include the possible as well as the actual; and in the second place, we are considering the real to include mathematical entities, as well as "real beings" (*entia*) in the more proper sense of that term. Our justification for this is that whereas mathematical entities may well be mere beings of reason (*entia rationis*), they at least are not objects of second intention as are logical entities. Hence relations that fall within the province of mathematics may be considered as being real relations, at least in contrast to properly logical relations. . . .

vestigation of such relations pertains to logic involves, from the Aristotelian point of view, a profound confusion of the logical with the real.

Nor would it make any difference that before such relational forms can enter as constituents into so-called logical proposi- tions, it is necessary first to abstract from the concreteness of temporal priority or geometrical congruence. On the contrary, the mere fact that a relation is considered in general and apart from the specific differences contained under that genus—or to put the same point in language more congenial to modern logi- cians, the mere fact that a formal system is taken as unin- terpreted and in abstraction from its possible interpretations— this mere fact certainly does not indicate that what is thus being considered is any less real as a relation or as a possible structural pattern, according to which things might really be ordered *in rerum natura.*

In other words, the point would seem to be that on the Aristo- telian view, the proper subject matter of logic is to be deter- mined not by any mere distinction of the abstract from the con- crete or of the general from the specific,[8] but rather by a distinc- tion of the intentional from the non-intentional. On the other hand, since the mathematical logician would seem to be willing to accept mere generality of relational forms and mere freedom from content as an adequate criterion of the logical, it follows that for the mathematical logician logic must cease to be a mere *organon* in the Aristotelian sense, and must become instead a general science of relations, of real relations quite as much as logical relations. Indeed, we wonder if such is not precisely the import of that grandiose scheme of a *speciosa generalis,* which was originally envisaged by Leibniz and which would have for its objective nothing less than the determination of a "universal system of possible orders" or of possible "forms of connection in general." [9]

---

[8] In other words, we are suggesting that the formalism of modern logic amounts to no more than a consideration of forms in abstraction from content, i.e., of the generic in abstraction from all specific differences.

[9] These expressions are Cassirer's (v. *Substance and Function* [Chicago 1923], pp. 92-93). In fact, our general interpretation of the import of formalism in mod- ern logic is, we suggest, not unlike Cassirer's.

Nor can it be said that in so characterizing the formalism of mathematical logic, we are deliberately foisting upon it a kind of Platonic realism—as if the mathematical logicians actually presupposed the existence of a vast array of relational forms and patterns laid up in some Platonic heaven. True, mathematical logic would seem to be entirely patient of an interpretation in terms of a Platonic metaphysics. And not a few of the older mathematical logicians would seem actually to have placed some such interpretation upon it.[10] And yet regardless of whether one interprets mathematical logic in this light or not, the import of its formalism would appear to be not other than what we have represented it as being.

For suppose one takes the extreme position that the forms considered in mathematical logic have no other foundation than arbitrary human convention, it would still be the case that such forms would not be regarded otherwise than as possible relational structures. Only this time, these structures will not be anchored in a Platonic world of forms, but rather in the more currently fashionable domain of the analytic and the tautologous. Indeed, if, to borrow Professor Blanshard's happy phrasing, you "confront ultimate problems" with nothing more "in your box of tools than mathematics and sense data," inevitably the patterns and types of order that you ascribe to your sense data will have already been determined *a priori* in the analytic propositions of your mathematics and/or logic.

Hence so far as the contrast with Aristotelian logic is concerned, a conventional formalism amounts to just about the same thing as a Platonic formalism. For whereas the Platonist talks about a world of forms, the conventionalist talks about the analytic. And whereas the Platonist talks of a sense world in which the formal structures of logic receive concrete exemplification, the conventionalist talks about the domain of synthetic propositions. But to Platonist and conventionalist alike, a formal logic means a logic of forms, and a logic of forms means a logic of relations, and a logic of relations means a science of

---

[10] Notably, Eaton, Cohen, and even, to an extent, Russell in the *Principles of Mathematics.*

the most general types of structure, order, and connection. In contrast, to the Aristotelian logician such a logic of forms or relations involves a serious confusion of intentional forms with non-intentional forms, of logical relations with real relations, and hence of logic with mathematics and possibly also ontology.

But our task is still far from complete. For granted that the formalism of modern logic is what we say it is, and granted that the Aristotelian logician would criticize such formalism on the ground of its involving a confusion of intentional forms with non-intentional forms, one will still want to know just how and on what basis the Aristotelian effects his distinction between the intentional and the non-intentional. True, examples may make the distinction superficially plausible, but they scarcely explain it. Thus one might acknowledge that there was a certain sense in which relations of linear congruence or temporal priority might be real relations, whereas relations of predicate to subject, or of middle term to extremes, etc., might be only relations of reason. That is to say, in the case of the former type of relation, one readily recognizes that a human being can perfectly well be before another in time, really and *in rerum natura* and quite independently of any human cognitive operations. On the other hand, that a predicate should be related to its subject, or a universal to its instances, or a middle term to its extremes—all of these are clearly not relations which hold in the real world; and insofar as such relations exist at all—and they certainly do exist—they exist only in the context of human thought and cognition.

And yet just how is one to tell, and just what criterion is one to use to determine, when a relation is a mere logical relation and not a real relation. In answer, we should like to suggest that a so-called logical relation or relation of reason is always a relation of identity. Now unhappily, the term "identity" is a term used in many different senses in philosophy. However, we hope that we can make clear how, in the sense in which we are using it,[11] identity is a relation such that it can only be "of

_____

[11] It should become apparent from the context that our sense of "identity" differs alike from the sense in which idealistic logicians sometimes use the term,

reason," and never a real relation *in rerum natura,* and also how identity is a relation that is exclusively adapted to provide that peculiar feature of intentionality which, as we have suggested, is essential to all logical entities on the Aristotelian view.

But first as to intentionality. Doubtless, it is well known that in the tradition of classical realism, the cognitive relation (which is simply the relation of intentionality) is necessarily a relation of identity. For after all, the basic thesis of the realist is that knowledge means knowledge of real things themselves, and as they are in themselves. Accordingly, no mere relation of similarity, after the fashion of the copy theory, would suffice for this purpose. Still less would the requirements of realism be met by any theory holding that the object of knowledge, in being known, had in some way or other to be changed or partially constructed in and through the cognitive process. This would lead straight to idealism in some form or other. In consequence, the relation of identity would seem to be the only one appropriate to the peculiar phenomenon of cognition. So, too, those logical instruments of cognition—terms, propositions, and arguments—which, as we have already suggested, are nothing but intentions, would presumably also have to be nothing but relations of identity.

So much, then, may suffice by way of indicating the intimate connection between identity and logical intentionality. But what, now, of our contention that identity can only be a relation of reason, and never a real relation? In support of this, we need but remark that a thing[12] can be identical only with itself and not with something else. Yet in order for a thing to be identified with itself, it must in some sense or other be separated or divided from itself—after all, identity is a two-term relation: for x to enter into a relation of identity, it must be identified with something. Accordingly, the exigencies of the relation are such that a thing must first be separated from itself in order to be identi-

and from the sense in which mathematical logicians use it. With the latter, "identity" is usually confined to the notion of an identity between two individuals, and is never, so far as we know, employed to signify the relation of a universal to its instances. . . .

[12] Needless to say, this word is here to be taken in its full analogical import, and not merely in the sense of "substance."

fied with itself. But clearly, nothing can ever really and in fact be actually divided from itself, so that it enters into a real relation of identity with itself. On the other hand, what cannot be effected in fact and in reality can be achieved intellectually and by reason. For reason can separate in thought what is really but one in fact; and having thus separated what is not separate really, reason can then recombine such rationally, but not really, separated parts. In other words, a relation of identity is precisely an achievement of reason.

Nevertheless, granting that the relation of identity is a relation of reason, what now remains to be shown is that such typical logical entities as concepts, propositions, syllogisms, etc., are nothing but relations of identity. In short, what we want now to show is not only that reason or intelligence *can* effect a relation of identity, but that in its efforts to understand it always *does* do so. Identity, that is to say, is the indispensable means or instrument of human knowledge.

Accordingly, let us proceed at once to a consideration of universal concepts and propositions to see if, in fact, they are but relations of identity. And first as to concepts. Surely, it will be admitted that without them there can be no such thing as knowledge, assuming, that is, that an extreme nominalism is simply untenable. But just what is a universal? Of course, one can try to make of it a kind of subsistent entity, existing in its own right. But, then, one is faced with all the difficulties or perplexities of an extreme realism of the Platonic type. Or as another alternative, one can insist that a universal is something that is wholly and without qualification of the mind. And in a sense, of course, this is true. Yet unless one is very careful, one may take it in the wrong sense, and then it becomes quite unintelligible how a universal concept can ever be legitimately applied to real things or truly predicated of them. Thus we say, "That is a tree," and we mean that it is a tree really and in fact. And yet how could it be a tree really, if "tree" were only something in the mind and of reason, and not real at all? In short, on such an interpretation we are up against all the difficulties of conceptualism.

Why not, then, try an altogether different alternative? Instead of trying to make of a universal a kind of atomic, self-contained thing existing either just in a Platonic realm or just in the mind, why not treat it as a relation, and more specifically as a relation of identity? So considered, the universal "tree" would be simply a relation of identity between particular, individual trees and what they are, i.e., their essential nature. On such a basis, it then becomes understandable how "tree" can be predicated of an individual, in the sense that one can say of the latter that it *is* the former.

Further, if we remind ourselves how a relation of identity involves a dividing of a thing from itself and a consequent reidentification of the thing with itself, we can see how this is precisely what happens in the case of the universal. For in an existing individual thing its "what" and its "that," its essence and its supposit are one. But intellectually, we are able to divide "tree" from that which is a tree; and having thus separated the "what" or essence from the "that," we can in turn reidentify them in the proposition, "That is a tree."

And now from this exhibition of the concept as simply a relation of identity, we are in a position to see how a proposition too is but a relation of identity in its turn. For it is simply because a universal concept is a relation of identity that it is, as we say, predicable of the particulars to which it is so related. Hence actually to predicate such a universal of a subject is actually to identify it with one or more of those particulars to which it stands in a relation of identity. In short, to say that S is P is not to assert that S is included in P, or is a member of P, or is equal to P, or is an argument of the function P; instead, it involves nothing more nor less than the identification of the predicate concept with the subject.

Moreover, in support of this contention that a proposition is but a relation of identity between subject and predicate, we shall add one further piece of evidence and shall try to remove one possible source of misunderstanding. As for the evidence, it consists in the simple fact, familiar to all students of logic, that in predication one cannot predicate a part of a whole, but only a whole of a whole. This, we suggest, is simply because it being necessary to identify the predicate with the subject, it is impossible to consider the predicate as related to the subject in the manner of part to whole.

For instance, one cannot say that a man is his two legs, but one can say that he is two-legged. Or, again, if one considers that man's essence is a composite essence of matter and form (body and soul),[13] one cannot say that man is his reason or intelligence, but only that man is rational or intelligent; nor can one say that man is his animal body, but only that he is an animal. Now it will be remembered that Aquinas[14] explains this on the ground that the soul being a real physical part (in the sense of form) of the human being, it cannot be predicated of the human being, on the other hand, the differentia, "rational," though it be derived from the form and based on the form, is not the form, and hence can be predicated of man. The reason for this is that concepts such as "rational," "animal," and "two-legged," although they are based on what is only a part of the whole man (whether essence or individual), nevertheless mean or signify the whole;[15] hence they can be predicated of it in the sense of being identified with it, it being possible to identify only a whole with a whole, never a part with a whole.

So much, then, for the item of supporting evidence. What, now, of the possible source of misunderstanding regarding this interpretation of the proposition as being but a relation of identity? We suggest that the misunderstanding is likely to arise from

---

[13] These examples are drawn from the Thomistic account of the composition that is supposed to be present in the essences of mere natural objects. However, such examples are used only for purposes of illustration. We feel sure that our argument must be regarded as conclusive, regardless of whether one agrees with the philosophy implied in the examples or not.

[14] Cf. *De Ente et Essentia,* Chs. II and III.

[15] "The genus, then, signifies indeterminately everything in the species. It does not indicate the matter alone. Similarly, the difference also signifies the whole and does not indicate merely the form. . . . The genus signifies the whole as a name expressing what is material in the thing without the proper form's determination. The genus, then, is taken from the matter, even though it is not matter. . . . Difference, however, signifies the whole as a name taken in a definite way from the form, without determinate matter being included in its primary notion." *On Being and Essence* by St. Thomas Aquinas, translated with an Introduction and Notes by A. A. Maurer (Toronto, 1949), p. 35.

one's supposing that, because of the requirement of an identity between S and P, therefore predication can never involve more than the mere assertion that S is S. And yet such would quite clearly be a misunderstanding, for, certainly, to say that man is rational or is animal or is two-legged is very different from saying that man is man.

True, one can predicate S of S, just as one can predicate P of S. Moreover, in both cases one has to do simply with a relation of identity. Not only that, but it being a strict relation of identity that is involved in each case, one must also recognize that the prior distinction in each case—i.e., the distinction of P from S, as well as the distinction of S from S, is only a distinction of reason—i.e., a distinction that is effected simply by the intellect, and in no wise a distinction between things that are distinct really and *in rerum natura.*

And yet even though it is only a distinctio of reason in both cases, still the distinction of P from S is different from the distinction of S from S. For the former, while it is a distinction of reason, is at the same time a distinction with a certain foundation in reality, whereas the latter is a distinction of reason purely and simply.[16] And if one asks what the real distinction is that founds the distinction of reason in the case of "S is P," we have already given some intimation as to the correct answer. For when one says "Man is rational" or "Man is animal," the distinction of P from S is in each case founded on the real distinctness of the parts of the essence "man," *viz.,* form and matter, or rational soul and animal body. Likewise, when one says that "Man is two-legged," the distinction of predicate from subject is founded on the real distinction of accident from substance.

Nonetheless, even though the distinction of P from S is founded on a real distinction, it is itself but a distinction of reason and the consequent predication of P of S is a relation of identity. For as we have already noted, whatever the real foundation of the difference between predicate and subject, one has to say "Man is two-legged," not "Man is the accident of two-

---

[16] The Scholastic terminology here would be *distinctio rationis ratiocinatae,* in contrast to *distinctio rationis ratiocinantis.*

leggedness"; or "Man is rational," not "Man is a rational soul," etc.

So much, then, for the Aristotelian account of the proposition as involving but a relation of identity.[17] It is precisely this relation of identity that is the source of the radical intentionality of the Aristotelian proposition. And it is precisely this intentionality that necessitates, on the Aristotelian view, a clear distinction of intentions from things intended: for while the latter may be real relations, the former can only be relations of reason. Now this does not mean that such real relational forms cannot be investigated at all; it only means that it is not the proper business of logic to investigate them, but rather of mathematics and perhaps metaphysics. And although, in such mathematical and metaphysical investigations, it is necessary to use logical or intentional relations as tools or instruments, still these purely logical relations must not be confused with the real relations which it is their business upon occasion to intend or represent.

Nevertheless, if our main thesis is correct, it is precisely such a confusion that is involved in the formalism of modern mathematical logic. Accordingly, in order to clinch our argument, we must needs consider briefly the theory of the proposition as that has been developed in mathematical logic, to see whether in fact there is implicit in it such a confusion of the logical with the real as we have been suggesting.

Now as is well known, the modern theory of the proposition really grows out of a sharp critique of the older Aristotelian theory. And the trouble with the older theory, so the mathematical logicians say, is that it wishes to treat all propositions as involving the simple S — P form. However, this entails much needless strait-jacketing and even distortion, in the case of propositions that involve many-termed relations.

For instance, consider the following propositions:

Socrates was human.

---

[17] In this short paper we cannot attempt to show how the syllogism, too, is a relation of identity, and as such an intention, quite as much as the concept and the proposition. Nevertheless, an adequate defense of our thesis would necessitate our exhibiting the contrast between formalism and intentionality in the sphere of argument, as well as in that of the proposition.

Socrates was the teacher of Plato.

Socrates took the hemlock from the jailer.

Now to treat all three of these as having the same S — P form is palpably absurd, say the mathematical logicians. Instead, it is far better to represent the structural form of propositions through the device of so-called propositional functions. According to such a scheme, the first proposition in the above list would be an instance of a one-place function, the second of a two-place function, the third of a three-place function, etc.[18] By such a technique of analysis, so the modern logicians argue, the many-termed character of the vast majority of relations can be adequately dealt with, and will not have to be simply glossed over, as is done in the simple subject-predicate treatment.

But already such a criticism of the Aristotelian theory is pregnant with that confusion of the logical with real which we are attempting to disclose. For consider how an Aristotelian would reply to such an attack. Thus with reference to the examples cited, he would insist that he was entirely willing to recognize that the relations which the real substance, Socrates, entered into with Plato, or with his own human nature, or with his jailer, or with the hemlock, etc., were real relations. Not only that, but each of them is a very different relation from each of the others; and no one of them is in any sense reducible to the others. And as for the notion that *all* three of these relations are reducible to the subject-predicate relation, no Aristotelian would ever maintain this, for the simple reason that on the Aristotelian view *no one* of these relations is a relation of subject to predicate. On the contrary, the relation of an individual substance to its nature or essence, or the relation of teacher to student, or the relation of taking something from someone— these are all real relations[19] and not logical relations at all.

---

[18] For our present purposes, it will suffice if we confine our investigation to so-called atomic propositions exclusively.

[19] It should be noted that although all of these relations are real relations, they are not all real relations of the same kind: whereas the two latter relations are instances of regular predicamental relations, the first is an instance of a transcendental relation. However, this distinction, though extremely important in itself, is of no particular concern to our present argument.

Nevertheless, when it comes to a question of knowing such real relations, or of grasping them intellectually, then the Aristotelian would insist that logic would have to be used and that the instrument of logic could be none other than the intentional relation of identity. Thus, for instance, if one wants to know what the relation of congruence is, one has to use a predicate to describe it; and the relation of that predicate to its subject will be one of identity. And yet this relation of identity will in this case *intend* not itself, but rather the relation of congruence.

And so also with any other relation, for instance the relation x R y, as that might be defined by postulates of, say, symmetry, transitivity and reflexivity. If one asks about such a relation and wants to know something about it, the answer or answers must be in terms of propositions in which one will assert certain things about the relation x R y. That is to say, these propositions will be of the S — P form and will involve the relation of identity between subject and predicate. But still they will not be proposition's *about* the relation of identity; nor will they have the effect of *reducing* a generalized relation of congruence to a mere relation of subject to predicate.

Or likewise, if one wants to know about an individual, say Socrates, the only way one can do so is to use predicates that will describe Socrates, and that will be related to the subject "Socrates" by a relation of identity. And this will be true even if a given predicate signifies a certain predicamental relation that Socrates stands in to someone else—say, that of being the teacher of Plato. Nevertheless, to identify "teacher of Plato" with "Socrates" does not mean that one is identifying the real relation as such with Socrates. After all, one does not say "Socrates is (or was) the relation 'teacher of Plato.'" Nor does such identification of predicate with subject mean that one is reducing the real relation of Socrates to Plato to a mere subject-predicate relationship. On the contrary, Socrates is (or was) really and in fact related to Plato as his teacher. We come to know the fact of this relation through an entirely different relation, *viz.,* the intentional relation of identity between subject and predicate.

However, that such a logical or intentional relation should never be confused with the real relation which it represents is something which the mathematical logicians never seem able to grasp. Thus when they analyze a proposition such as "Socrates took the hemlock from the jailer," and say that it involves a propositional function with three arguments, rather than an identification of a predicate term with a subject, what they are really doing, it would seem, is analyzing not the *proposition* at all, but rather the *real situation* in which Socrates found himself just prior to his death.

*   *   *

GILBERT RYLE

Waynflete Professor of Metaphysical Philosophy in the University of Oxford.

Ryle belongs to that philosophical school which outsiders call "linguistic philosophy," and which insiders declare is neither linguistic nor a school, but plain philosophy in the tradition of Socrates and Aristotle.

There has emerged in English philosophy in the twentieth century a rather pervasive conviction that most philosophical problems lie not so much in reality but in our verbal descriptions of it. Consider: *if I burned the steak last night then it was true a hundred years ago that I was going to do it, and thus I couldn't help it.* Now the current conviction in England is that the way out of such an intellectual trap is never to be had either through a comprehensive metaphysics of fatalism or freedom, or by calling in the inevitably distorting aid of purely formal logic. Rather—as a first approximation—the conviction is that inquiring into the uses of the word "true," for example, is more fruitful than inquiring about something called the nature of truth.

Further elaborated, this view is that logic applies to words as well as to whole arguments. For example, it is part of the (informal) logic of the word "nephew" that precludes me from speaking of my female nephew. Still further elaborated, with Ryle's own words from another place: "live problems of Informal Logic are forced upon us willy-nilly by the interferences which are unwittingly committed between different teams of ideas." My dismal reflections on yesterday's steak would be such an interference and, on this view, so would Aristotle's discussion of the sea battle tomorrow.

The following selection is taken from the last essay of a short book in which Ryle had applied his approach to a number of specific problems. Here he discusses what he calls a boundary dispute between the philosopher and the formal logician. The influences which the view described above have upon philosophical writing are abundantly evidenced. First, both the informal logic, which Ryle defends, and the formal logic, which he eschews, are conceived (in contrast with most of the other authors in this volume) as being quite remarkably independent from any broader metaphysical theories of philosophy. Secondly, philosophical insights are conveyed obliquely, by example and analogy, by shock and suggestion, and, especially with Ryle, by a wildly galloping army of metaphors.

FORMAL AND INFORMAL LOGIC[1]

* * *

Since Aristotle, there has existed a branch of inquiries, often entitled 'Formal Logic,' which has always adhered more or less closely to general philosophical inquiries. It is not easy to describe this liaison between Formal Logic and philosophy. The systematic presentation of the rules of syllogistic inference is a very different sort of activity from, say, the elucidation of the concept of pleasure. The Aristotle who inaugurated the former is the same thinker as the Aristotle who considerably developed the latter, yet the kinds of thinking in which he was involved are very widely different. The technical problems in the theory of the syllogism have a strong resemblance to the problems of Euclidean geometry; the ideals of systematization and rigorous proof are at work, questions of switches and shades of significance are barred, false moves are demonstrable fallacies. The problems in, say, the theory of pleasure or perception or moral responsibility are not like this. Aristotle debates with Plato and Socrates, and the issues become better defined as the debate progresses, but the debate does not take the shape of a chain of theorems, nor do the arguments used in that debate admit of notational codification. Whether a given philosophical

---

[1] Reprinted from Gilbert Ryle, *Dilemmas* (New York: Cambridge University Press, 1954).

argument is valid or fallacious is, in general, itself a debatable question. Simple inspection cannot decide. More often it is a question of whether the argument has much, little or no force. Yet different though Formal Logic is from philosophy, the operations characteristic of Formal Logic exercise a detectable, if minor, control over the operations characteristic of philosophy. For good or for ill, the ways in which Aristotle debates the notion of *pleasure,* the *soul* or the *continuum* reflect lessons which he had taught himself in his logical inquiries. Nor is Aristotle peculiar in this. With a negligible number of exceptions, every philosopher of genius and nearly every philosopher of even high talent from Aristotle to the present day has given himself some schooling in some parts of Formal Logic, and his subsequent philosophical reasonings have exhibited the effects upon him of this self-schooling, including sometimes his revolts against it.

In some respects the following analogy holds. Fighting in battles is markedly unlike parade-ground drill. The best conducted drill-evolutions would be the worst possible battle-movements, and the most favourable terrain for a rearguard action would entirely forbid what the barrack-square is made for. None the less the efficient and resourceful fighter is also the well-drilled soldier. The ways in which he takes advantage of the irregularities of the ground show the marks of the schooling he had received on the asphalt. He can improvise operations in the dark and at the risk of his life now, partly because he had learned before to do highly stereotyped and formalized things in broad daylight and in conditions of unmitigated tedium. It is not the stereotyped motions of drill, but its standards of perfection of control which are transmitted from the parade-ground to the battlefield.

Aristotelian Formal Logic gave weapon-drill in only a limited variety of rather short-range inference-weapons. The supplementations given by the Megarian and Stoic logicians were, unfortunately, only slightly and belatedly influential. It was left to the nineteenth and twentieth centuries to generalize and systematize the discipline. In particular, the discipline was then in considerable measure mathematicized, and mathematicized in two separate ways. First, the new builders of Formal Logic, being themselves mathematicians, knew how to give mathematical shape, mathematical rigour and mathematical notations to this branch of abstract theory. Secondly, since their interest in Formal Logic derived from dissatisfaction with the logical foundations of mathematics itself, Formal Logic came to be not only mathematical in style but also mathematical in subject-matter; to be employed, that is, primarily in order to fix the logical powers of the terms or concepts on which hinged the proofs of propositions in pure mathematics.

Formal or Symbolic Logic has grown up into a science or discipline of such scope, such rigour and such fertility that it is now out of all danger of surviving only as the nursery-governess of philosophy. Indeed, philosophers are now complacent if they and their pupils are capable of doing their schoolroom sums in the subject, and gratified and flattered if original logicians are willing to join them, from time to time, in their own expeditions over the moors.

Now, perhaps, I can indicate in a very provisional way the nature of the dispute which has already begun between Formal Logic and general philosophy. Some properly zealous, if sometimes gratuitously jealous Formal Logicians are now beginning to say to the philosopher 'It is time that you stopped trying to solve your problems by your old-fashioned exercises in improvisation and trial-and-error. Your problems are, as you say yourself, logical problems, and we have now got the procedures for solving logical problems. Where you grope, we calculate. Where you haggle, we employ the cash-register. Where you ponder imponderable pros and cons, we work out the correct logical change.'

The natural response of the offended and also jealous philosopher is this. 'Yes, you have invented or hit upon a private game, with fewer pieces but more squares than are provided by chess. You have converted the words "logic" and "logical" to your private ends, and now you invite us to cease exploring the moors in order to become conductors on your trams. And for what? For nothing, apparently, but the proliferation of truistic

formulae. No philosophical problem of any interest to anyone
has yet been solved by reducing it to the shape or size that suits
some slot in your slot-machine. Your cash-register is indeed quite
impeccable and totally neutral, and for that reason it cannot be
appealed to for aid in the settlement of any bargaining-disputes.
There was the notion, once projected by Leibniz and later
championed by Russell, that philosophers would soon be so
equipped and drilled that they would be able to decide their
issues by calculation. But now we have learned, what we should
have foreseen, that questions which can be decided by calculation are different, *toto caelo* different, from the problems that
perplex. There is one person to whom it is impertinence to give
the advice that he should keep one foot on the kerb—and that
is the pathfinder. Kerbs cannot exist where the road is unmade,
and roads cannot be made where the route has not been found.'

You can guess for yourselves the abusive nouns which are
now liable to be interchanged. 'Muddler-through,' 'romantic,'
'anti-scientist,' 'hunch-rider,' 'litterateur' and of course 'Platonist' come from the one side; from the other side there come 'Formalist,' 'computer,' 'reductionist,' 'pseudo-scientist' and, of
course, 'Platonist.'

As might be anticipated, neither party is right, though both
are more nearly right than the appeasers who try to blend the
operations of the one party with the operations of the other.
The drill-sergeant is wrong who thinks that soldiering consists
in going through the motions tabulated in the drill-book. The
franc-tireur is wrong who thinks that soldiering consists in out-
bursts of amateur gunmanship. But neither is so wrong as the
scenario-writer who represents fighting soldiers as heroes going
berserk in close column of platoons.

Let us examine, rather more closely, the actual work, as distinct from the intermittent promises of Formal Logicians. Aristotle, it is nearly enough correct to say, examined certain ranges
of inferences, namely those which pivot on the notions of *all,*
some, and *not.* He saw that from two premisses like 'some men
are blue-eyed' and 'some men are red-haired' it does not follow
that any men are both blue-eyed and red-haired, or, of course,

that none are. On the other hand from 'all men are mortal' and 'all philosophers are men' it does follow that all philosophers are mortal. There are rules governing the employment of *all, some* and *not* such that all inferences pivoting on two or all three of these concepts, arranged in certain ways, are valid, while all inferences pivoting on them arranged in certain other ways are invalid. These rules are perfectly general, anyhow in this sense, that differences of concrete subject-matter make no difference to the validity or fallaciousness of the inferences. The quantifier-words 'all' and 'some' can be followed indifferently by 'men,' 'cows,' 'gods' or what you will, without affecting our decision that the inference holds or does not hold. What determines whether a proposed syllogism is valid or fallacious is the work given to 'all,' 'some' and 'not,' irrespective of the concrete topics of its premisses and conclusion. So, for brevity, we can say that Aristotle was investigating the logical powers of certain topic-neutral concepts, namely those of *all, some* and *not.* These are sometimes listed among what are nowadays called the 'logical constants.'

In a similar way the Megarian and Stoic logicians began the investigation of the logical powers of the equally topic-neutral concepts of *and, or,* and *if;* they concentrated on certain propositional conjunctions or connectives, where Aristotle had concentrated on certain quantifiers. They were studying the legitimacy and illegitimacy of possible arguments in so far as they hinged on these particular topic-neutral conjunctions.

These studies yielded a modest degree of codification of the inference-patterns that were examined, and even a semi-Euclideanization of the rules of these inferences. Certain crucial fallacy-patterns were classified. So it was natural, though, as we now know, quite mistaken to suppose that any piece of valid reasoning whatsoever was, by some device or other of rewording, reducible to one of the already scheduled patterns, and every piece of fallacious reasoning reducible to one of the already registered howlers. Some terms like 'all,' 'some' and 'not,' and perhaps also 'and,' 'or' and 'if' do carry inferences; the rest, it was mistakenly supposed, do not.

Part of what characterizes the terms which do, on this view, carry inferences is that these terms or 'logical constants' are indifferent to subject-matter or are topic-neutral; so part of what characterizes all the other terms which were supposed not to carry inferences is that they are not topic-neutral. Inferences are valid or invalid in virtue of their forms, and to say this, it was supposed, was to say that they were valid or invalid because of the ways in which certain topic-neutral or purely formal expressions occurred in certain positions and arrangements in their premisses and conclusions. This temptingly crisp doctrine, whose obituary notice has yet to be written, might easily suggest the following demarcation of Formal Logic from philosophy. Formal Logic, it might be said, maps the inference-powers of the topic-neutral expressions or logical constants on which our arguments pivot; philosophy has to do with the topical or subject-matter concepts which provide the fat and the lean, but not the joints or the tendons of discourse. The philosopher examines such notions as *pleasure, colour, the future,* and *responsibility,* while the Formal Logician examines such notions as *all, some, not, if* and *or.*

But this way of making the division quickly breaks down. To begin with, topic-neutrality is not enough to qualify an expression as a logical constant. European languages, ancient and modern, and especially the largely uninflected languages, are rich in topic-neutral expressions, most of which have, for very good reasons, received no attention at all from Formal Logicians. We may call English expressions 'topic-neutral' if a foreigner who understood them, but only them, could get no clue at all from an English paragraph containing them what that paragraph was about. Such expressions can or must occur in any paragraph about any topic, abstract or concrete, biographical or legal, philosophical or scientific. They are not dedicated to this topic as distinct from that. They are like coins which enable one to bargain for any commodity or service whatsoever. You cannot tell from the coins in the customer's hand what he is going to buy. In this way 'not,' 'and,' 'all,' 'some,' 'a,' 'the,' 'is,' 'is a member of,' etc., certainly are topic-neutral, but so are 'several,' 'most,' 'few,' 'three,' 'half,' 'although,' 'because,' 'perhaps,' 'may,' as well as hosts of other conjunctions, particles, prepositions, pronouns, adverbs, etc. Some expressions seem to be nearly but not quite topic-neutral. The temporal conjunctions 'while,' 'after' and 'before,' and the spatial conjunction 'where' could be used not in all, but only in nearly all sorts of discourse. Our foreigner could tell from the occurrence of temporal conjunctions in the paragraph that no purely geometrical matter was being discussed.

But not only do Formal Logicians very properly ignore the great majority of topic-neutral expressions, as not being in their beat; they also, very properly, bestow their professional attentions upon the logical powers of certain classes of expressions which are by no means topic-neutral. Relational expressions like 'north of,' 'taller than' and 'encompasses' are pivots of strict inferences, and it has proved necessary and feasible to divide such expressions up into families according to the sorts of inferences which they do and do not carry. 'Taller-than,' for example, is transitive, in the sense that if A is taller than B, and B than C, then A is taller than C. But 'next to' and 'mother of' are not transitive. A can be next to B and B to C without A being next to C; and Sarah cannot be the mother of the child of her own daughter. This does not prevent us from discovering rigorous parities of reasoning between, for example, inferences hinging on 'north of' and inferences hinging on 'encompasses.' But the feature of parity cannot always be detached for separate examination by publication of some elided topic-neutral expression. Sometimes it can. 'Fatter than' works, in some directions, like 'hotter than,' and what is common to the two can be brought out by the rewording 'more fat than' and 'more hot than,' where the expression 'more so and so than' is a detachable topic-neutral expression.

So we should say, perhaps, with considerable loss of crispness and misleadingness, that Formal Logic is a certain sort of study of parities of reasoning or certain special kinds of parities of reasoning; and that it is convenient, when possible, to exhibit these parities by operations with topic-neutral expressions detached from any particular topical contexts; but that this is not essential and is not always possible. Not all strict inferences pivot on the recognized logical constants, and not all topic-neutral expressions qualify for treatment as logical constants.

A further amendment is required. I have spoken as if our ordinary 'and,' 'or,' 'if,' 'all,' 'some' and so on are identical with the logical constants with which the Formal Logician operates. But this is not true. The logician's 'and,' 'not,' 'all,' 'some' and the rest are not our familiar civilian terms; they are conscript terms, in uniform and under military discipline, with memories, indeed, of their previous more free and easy civilian lives, though they are not living those lives now. Two instances are enough. If you hear on good authority that she took arsenic and fell ill you will reject the rumour that she fell ill and took arsenic. This familiar use of 'and' carries with it the temporal notion expressed by 'and subsequently' and even the causal notion expressed by 'and in consequence.' The logicians' conscript 'and' does only its appointed duty—a duty in which 'she took arsenic and fell ill' is an absolute paraphrase of 'she fell ill and took arsenic.' This might be called the minimal force of 'and.' In some cases the overlap between the military duties and the civilian work and play of an expression is even slighter. What corresponds in the glossary of Formal Logic to the civilian word 'if' is an expression which plays only a very small, though certainly cardinal part of the role or roles of that civilian word.

This point that Formal Logic operates (1) only with some, and not with all topic-neutral expressions, and (2) only with artificial extracts from the selected few topic-neutral expressions of ordinary discourse is sometimes used by philosophers as a criticism of the programme of Formal Logic. Where the philosopher concerns himself with full-blooded concepts like that of *pleasure* or *memory,* the Formal Logician concerns himself only with meatless concepts like those of *not* and *some*; and even these have to be filed down to reduced size and unnatural shape before the Formal Logician will deign to inspect them. Moreover, the philosopher investigates concepts which, in one way or another, generate genuine perplexities. He investigates the concept, say, of *seeing* and not that of, say, *perspiring,* since the former is charged with paradoxes where the latter is not. But, the criticism goes, the Formal Logician investigates the inference-carrying labours of concepts which engender no paradoxes whatsoever; what he finds out about *and* and *not* are only elaborations of what every child has completely mastered in his early talking years.

I mention this allegation here because it makes the right opening for me. It is quite false that doing Formal Logic is doing gratuitous and profitless philosophy upon philosophically transparent concepts. It is quite false, equally, that the philosopher is doing makeshift and amateurish Formal Logic upon wrongly chosen because non-logical concepts. The battlefield is not a makeshift parade-ground; and the parade-ground is not a sham battlefield.

None the less, there remains a very important way in which the adjective 'logical' is properly used to characterize both the inquiries which belong to Formal Logic and the inquiries which belong to philosophy. The Formal Logician really is working out the logic of *and, not, all, some,* etc., and the philosopher really is exploring the logic of the concepts of *pleasure, seeing, chance,* etc., even though the work of the one is greatly unlike the work of the other in procedure and in objectives. Neither is doing what the other is doing, much less is either doing improperly what the other is doing properly. Yet we are not punning when we say, for example, that the considerations which are decisive for both are 'logical' considerations, any more than we are punning if we say that the choice of drill-evolutions and the choice of battle-evolutions are both decided by 'military' considerations. How can this be?

I find the following partial parallel of some assistance. Trading begins with barter of goods for goods, and, by means of fixed places and times for markets, such barter-dealings can reach a fairly high degree of systematization. Though the relative exchange-values of different sorts of goods vary with times and places, some measure of stabilization can be achieved by tacit or explicit convention. There is, however, even at this stage, a strong pressure upon traders to use just a few kinds of consumable goods not only for consumption, but also, at least for a short time, as a sort of informal currency. Dried fishes, cigarettes or iron bars, though wanted for use, come also to be wanted because any other trader can be relied on to accept them, whether he himself wants to use them or not, because they will always be exchangeable anywhere for consumable goods. So long as they are reasonably imperishable, easy to store and handle, easy to count or weigh, and certain to be wanted some day by someone for consumption purposes, they are negotiable as exchange-tokens. From this stage to the stage of operating with a conventional currency or legal tender is a relatively short step. Though no one, perhaps, can be expected to want to use metal discs for any consumption purpose, everyone can be expected to want to use them for exchange-purposes. They might be described as auxiliary goods, goods which are of little or no utility in themselves, but of great utility for getting and disposing of other goods which are wanted for themselves.

For future purposes we should notice another kind of auxiliary goods. Baskets, pitchers, sacks, brown paper and string are, to exaggerate a little, of no use in themselves, but only for the collection and housing of goods which we do want for themselves. But clearly the way in which baskets and string are auxiliary to marketing and storing is different from the way in which coins are auxiliary. A basket or keg is only being actually useful to us when we are in possession of goods for it to contain. A coin is useful to us in another way. While we possess the coin, we do not possess what we shall buy with it. But still there is a certain similarity between them. A coin is commodity-neutral, for I can buy any sort of commodity with it. A sack or a piece of string is, in lower degree, commodity-neutral. You cannot tell from the fact that I go to market with a sack or some string precisely what kinds of goods I shall bring back with its aid. It would be useful for any of a fairly wide range of goods, though not, of course, for all kinds of goods.

Linguistic dealings between men have some of the features of market-dealings between men. There is a comparable pressure

upon language to evolve idioms, which may or may not be separate words, to subserve in stabilized ways different kinds of constantly recurring linguistic negotiations. We need and therefore
we get a variety of topic-neutral words, inflections, construc-
tions, etc., some of which function rather like baskets, pitchers,
string and wrapping-paper, while others function rather like the
dried fishes, cigarettes or iron bars and, later on, rather like the
coins and currency notes, part or the whole of whose utility is
to serve as instruments of exchange.

There arises, I suppose, a special pressure upon language to
provide idioms of this latter kind, when a society reaches the
stage where many matters of interest and importance to everyone have to be settled or decided by special kinds of talk. I
mean, for example, when offenders have to be tried and con-
victed or acquitted; when treaties and contracts have to be entered into and observed or enforced; when witnesses have to be
cross-examined; when legislators have to draft practicable meas-
ures and defend them against critics; when private rights and
public duties have to be precisely fixed; when complicated com-
mercial arrangements have to be made; when teachers have to
set tests to their pupils; and, by no means earliest, when theo-
rists have to consider in detail the strengths and weaknesses of
their own and one another's theories.

Those topic-neutral words of natural languages which are
nearest to the officially recognized logical constants roughly coincide, perhaps, with the best consolidated exchange-auxiliaries
that our native tongues have provided. They exist to be nego-
tiating instruments. The conscript expressions actually used by
Formal Logicians, together with the methodically designed expressions of mathematics, correspond in many respects with a
legal tender. A sentence with one or more 'logical words' in it,
is a sentence with one or more price-tickets on it. Other topic-
neutral words, inflections, etc., correspond more closely with
the paper, string, sacks and pitchers with which we go to and
return from the market.

Now perhaps we are in a position to see more clearly some of
the ways in which the Formal Logician's interests are unlike

those of the philosopher and yet not entirely separate. The ordinary person is much concerned both with the domestic or consumption-utility of different goods and also, as a marketer, with their exchange-values, i.e. what they can be got for or what they would fetch; and these considerations vary with every different kind and quantity of goods. No such problems exist for the bank clerk about the coins that he takes in and gives out. A sixpenny-bit buys whatever costs sixpence, and its purchasing power stands to the purchasing power of a penny or a half-crown in known and fixed relations. Its value is stamped on its face.

Somewhat similarly there is and can be no incertitude about the exchange-values of the numerals of simple arithmetic or the conscript logical constants of the Formal Logician, since they have been designed or chartered to do just what they do. Nor can there be much incertitude about the inference-carrying powers of such vernacular words as 'not,' 'some,' 'and' and 'or,' since their prime business is to make negotiations decidable.

Where the philosopher has to investigate both the special content of, say, the concepts of *enjoying* and *remembering* and their kinds of logical behaviour, the logician does not have to investigate his semi-technical concepts of *and* and *not*. Their work is what they are chartered to do, and he drew up their charters or at least has read them. On the other hand, a special theoretical task does remain for him to do. Much as arithmetic and algebra have problems of their own, which begin when the elementary use of numbers in counting is mastered, so the Formal Logician has his analogous problems, which begin long after the elementary mastery is achieved of his chartered *all, some* and *not; and, or, if* and the rest. His occupational problems are not how to determine the exchange-equivalents of his logical constants, but how to derive some from others, to establish, that is, the principles of the calculation of them. His task is to incorporate them in a sort of Euclidean deductive system. The experienced but uneducated bus-conductor could write down the beginning of an endless list of the correct change that can be given for different coins and handfuls of coins, but to do this would not be to do arithmetic. The accountant, unlike our bus-conductor, must know how to calculate, and some other experts must have developed the science which the accountant applies.

The topic-neutral expressions of our natural language which are the civilian counterparts to the conscript logical constants do not behave quite as their conscript counterparts behave, though the differences are sometimes slight and sometimes not troublesomely gross. For obvious reasons, logicians have conscripted only the soldierly-looking civilians and, as we have seen, there are good reasons why the languages of highly organized societies provide a certain number of decision-facilitating expressions.

But most of the terms of everyday and technical discourse are not like coins or even like cowrie-shells. They are like consumption-goods, which can, indeed, be traded for and traded with. But their barter-values are not stamped upon their faces. They can, for the most part, be the hinges of legitimate and illegitimate inferences; there are parities of reasoning between inferences pivoting on one of them and inferences pivoting on some others of them; but there is, ordinarily, no way of extracting from them some implicit logical constant or web of logical constants to be credited with the carriage of those inferences—any more than there is really an invisible half-crown lurking inside a bag of potatoes which renders these potatoes the barter-equivalent of a basket of fruit or a couple of lobsters.

They have their logical powers or barter-values, but they are not to be read off the terms of their official charters, since they have no charters. The philosopher's problem is to extract their logical powers from the dealings which we transact with them, somewhat as the phonetician has to extract the principles of phonetics from the ways in which we have learned to pronounce our words—though the method and purposes of the extraction are hugely different.

How then, it remains to be asked, is the philosopher a client of the Formal Logician? Part of the answer I have already suggested. To know how to go through completely stereotyped movements in artificial parade-ground conditions with perfect correctness is to have learned not indeed how to conduct one-self in battle but how rigorously to apply standards of soldierly efficiency even to unrehearsed actions and decisions in novel and nasty situations and in irregular and unfamiliar country.

Or, which is not quite the same thing, it is rather like what geometry is to the cartographer. He finds no Euclidean straight hedgerows or Euclidean plane meadows. Yet he could not map the sinuous hedgerows that he finds or the undulating meadows save against the ideally regular boundaries and levels in terms of which alone can he calculate out the relative positions and heights of the natural objects which he is to record from the visual observations that he makes. The cartographer is one of the clients of geometry. The possibility of his map being approximately correct or precise is the gift of Euclid. So is the possibility of his reading off his map distances, areas and bearings which he did not measure when constructing his map.

Or, lastly, it is what accountancy is to the merchant, who, though his problems are not arithmetical problems, still, in his handling of them, needs the constant back-room check of the properly balanced ledger. The trader is a client of the account-ant.

But patently fighting cannot be reduced to drill, cartography cannot be reduced to geometry, trading cannot be reduced to balancing accounts. Nor can the handling of philosophical problems be reduced to either the derivation or the application of theorems about logical constants. The philosopher is perforce doing what might be called 'Informal Logic,' and the suggestion that his problems, his results or his procedures should or could be formalized is as wildly astray as would be the corresponding suggestions about the soldier, the cartographer and the trader. We could go further and say that the whole point of drill, of geometry, of accountancy and of Formal Logic would be gone if they could be completely dissociated from their clients. It would be like reserving the roads for the sole use of steam-rollers, or like forbidding all trade save money-changing.

*   *   *